The Raintree Illustrated
Science Encyclopedia

6 $\dfrac{\text{DRU}}{\text{EVE}}$

The Raintree Illustrated

SCIENCE
ENCYCLOPEDIA

Raintree Publishers
Milwaukee · Toronto · Mexico City · Melbourne

Library of Congress Number: 83-11030

2   3   4   5   6   7   8   9   0   87   86   85   84

Printed in the United States of America.

Library of Congress Cataloging in Publication Data

Main entry under title:

The Raintree illustrated science encyclopedia.

   Bibliography: p. 1913
   Includes index.
   Summary: An encyclopedia of principles, concepts, and people in the
various fields of science and technology.
   1. Science — Dictionaries, Juvenile. [1. Science — Dictionaries]
I. Title: Illustrated science encyclopedia.
Q121.R34   1983   503.21   83-11030

ISBN 0-8172-2325-8 (set) trade
ISBN 0-8172-2331-2 (volume 6)

ISBN 0-8172-2300-2 (set) lib. bdg.
ISBN 0-8172-2306-1 (volume 6)

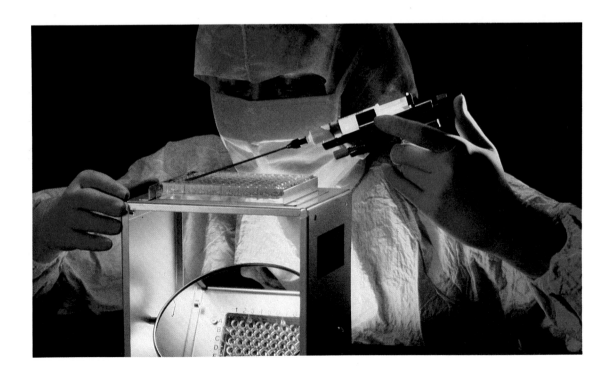

USING THE RAINTREE ILLUSTRATED
SCIENCE ENCYCLOPEDIA

You are living in a world in which science, technology, and nature are very important. You see something about science almost every day. It might be on television, in the newspaper, in a book at school, or in some other place. Often you want more information about what you see. *The Raintree Illustrated Science Encyclopedia* will help you find what you want to know. The Raintree encyclopedia has information on many science subjects. You may want to find out about mathematics, biology, agriculture, computer science, lasers, or rockets, for example. They are all in *The Raintree Illustrated Science Encyclopedia*. And there are many, many other subjects.

There are twenty volumes in the encyclopedia. The articles, which are called entries, are in alphabetical order through the first 19 volumes. On the spine of each volume, below the volume number, are some letters. The letters above the line are the first three letters of the first entry in that volume. The letters below the line are the first three letters of the last entry in that volume. In Volume 1, for example, you see that the first entry begins with **aar** and that the last entry begins with **arr**. Using the letters makes it easy to find the volume you need.

In the front of Volume 20, there are interesting projects that you can do on your own. The projects are fun to do, and they illustrate important science principles.

Also in Volume 20, there are two special features — an index and a bibliography. They are described in Volume 20.

Main Entries. The titles of the main entries in *The Raintree Illustrated Science Encyclopedia* are printed in capital letters. They look like this:
CAMERA.

The titles of some of the longer or more important entries are printed in larger capital letters.

At the beginning of each entry, you will see a phonetic pronunciation of the entry title. On page viii, there is a pronunciation key. Use it the same way you use your dictionary key.

At the end of each entry, there are two sets of initials. They look like this: S.R.G./W.R.S. The first set belongs to the person who wrote the entry. The

second set belongs to the special consultant who checked the entry for accuracy. Pages v and vi give you the names of all these people. Throughout the Raintree encyclopedia, measurements are given in both the metric and English systems.

Cross-References. Sometimes a subject has two names. The Raintree encyclopedia usually puts the information with the more common name. But in case you look up the less common name, there will be a cross-reference to tell you where to find the information. Suppose you wanted to look up something about the metric temperature scale. This scale is usually called the Celsius Scale. Sometimes, however, it is called the Centigrade Scale. The Raintree encyclopedia has the entry Celsius Scale. But if you had looked up Centigrade Scale, you would have found this: **CENTIGRADE SCALE** *See* CELSIUS SCALE. This kind of cross-reference tells you where to find the information you need.

There is another kind of cross-reference in the Raintree encyclopedia. It looks like this: *See* CLOUD. Or it looks like this: *See also* ELECTRICITY. These cross-references tell you where to find other helpful information on the subject you are reading about.

Projects. At the end of some entries, you will see this symbol ◥. That tells you that there is a project on that entry in Volume 20.

Illustrations. There are thousands of photos, charts, diagrams, and tables in the Raintree encyclopedia. They will help you better understand the entries you read. A caption describes each picture. Many of the pictures also have labels that point out important parts.

Index. The index lists every main entry by volume and page number. In addition, many subjects that are not main entries are also listed in the index.

Bibliography. In Volume 20, there is also a bibliography. The books in this list are on the same general subjects covered in the Raintree encyclopedia.

The Raintree Illustrated Science Encyclopedia was designed especially for you, the young reader. It is a source of knowledge for the world of science, technology, and nature. Enjoy it.

PRONUNCIATION GUIDE

These symbols have the same sound as the
darker letters in the sample words.

ə	balloon, ago	ō	cone, know
ər	learn, further	ȯ	all, saw
a	map, have	ȯi	boy, boil
ā	day, made	p	part, scrap
ä	father, car	r	root, tire
au̇	now, loud	s	so, press
b	ball, rib	sh	shoot, machine
ch	choose, nature	t	to, stand
d	did, add	th	thin, death
e	bell, get	<u>th</u>	then, this
ē	sweet, easy	ü	pool, lose
f	fan, soft	u̇	put, book
g	good, big	v	view, give
h	hurt, ahead	w	wood, glowing
i	rip, ill	y	yes, year
ī	side, sky	z	zero, raise
j	join, germ	zh	leisure, vision
k	king, ask		
l	let, cool		
m	man, same	'	strong accent
n	no, turn	'	weak accent

Drupes are fleshy fruits with single seeds, or stones. Typical drupes are shown above. The half cherry shows the drupe structure.

DRUPE (drüp) A drupe is a kind of fruit. Its seed is a single, stony pit. The seed is surrounded by juicy matter called the pulp, and is enclosed in a skin.

The best-known examples of the drupe are the plum, the cherry, the peach, and the apricot. Blackberries are made up of a number of small drupes called drupelets.

P.G.C./M.H.S.

DRY CLEANING (drī′ klēn′ ing) Dry cleaning is a process that removes dirt and stains from fabrics without the aid of water. Dry cleaning is not really "dry." Liquids such as perchloroethylene, or other petroleum solvents, are used in the process.

Dry cleaning plants handle mostly clothing. Some of them also clean draperies and rugs. Many clothes, including most of those made of wool, must be dry-cleaned to prevent shrinkage, fading, or other damage. Some materials, like vinyls and artificial leathers, should not be dry-cleaned because the process causes them to crack and split. Most garments contain labels that tell how the fabric should be cleaned.

Dry cleaning began in France in the late 1800s. The process was called French cleaning when it was first introduced into the United States in the early 1900s.

In a dry cleaning plant, garments are cleaned with others of the same color and type. A worker called a pre-spotter removes stains that would become permanent in the dry cleaning process. The garments are then put into a special washing machine, which consists of a moveable drum filled with cleaning fluid. Special soaps, or detergents, are usually added to the fluid to help in the cleaning process. The drum rotates and the fluid flows through the garments removing dirt and stains. Afterward the clothes are put into an extractor, which spins them at high speed to remove the fluid. Some dry cleaning plants have machines that do both the washing and extracting in the same unit. After the extraction process, the garments are placed in a dryer. The garments are tumbled around inside a rotating drum filled with warm air. This dries the garments.

A worker called a spotter uses chemicals and a steam gun, if necessary, to remove any remaining stains. A steam gun is a small, gun-shaped device. It shoots a jet of live steam onto a stain or spot. The hot steam helps loosen the particles of dirt. Next, the garments go to the presser, or finisher, who uses steam-operated pressing and shaping equipment to restore the garment to its original shape. The garments are then inspected. Small repairs are made, if necessary. They are hung on hangers and covered with plastic bags.

Self-service dry cleaning became popular in the U.S. in the 1960s. Dry cleaning machines, activated by coins, automatically clean and dry the clothes. Some of these self-service stores have special equipment that can be used to remove wrinkles and bad stains. Self-service dry cleaning is less expensive than the professional process. However, some materials require special handling, which can only be done by professionals.

The dry cleaning industry is one of the largest service industries in the U.S. There are about 25,000 dry cleaning plants, employing more than 250,000 people. In addition, many thousands of laundries accept clothes for dry cleaning, and then send the clothes to a dry cleaning plant. There are about 25,000 self-service dry cleaning stores in the U.S.

W.R.P./J.M.

DUCK (dək) Ducks are water birds related to the geese and swans. Some live in fresh water, near rivers and lakes, and in prairie and mountain marshes. Others live in coastal waters.

Ducks have short legs, webbed feet, and flattened beaks called bills. Their legs and webbed feet serve as paddles. Some bills have rough edges which the duck uses for sifting food from the water and the mud, and for holding fish. The ducks with shorter bills use them to pry off snails from rocks, and to pull clams off the bottom of a lake or pond.

There are two main kinds of ducks: the surface feeders and the diving ducks. The surface feeders eat by up-ending themselves in the water and leaving their tails sticking

out. The divers submerge and swim about under the water. Both are good flyers, once they get off the water and into the air. Surface feeders can fly directly into the air. Divers must flap across the water before they can become airborne.

The plumage of the duck consists of a layer of down feathers and a layer of waterproof feathers. The down is very fine and soft. It is next to the bird's skin and helps keep him warm. The outer feathers help keep the down layer dry. The outer feathers are covered with a waxy oil that comes from a gland at the base of the tail and is applied to the feathers with the bill. The male duck, called a drake, usually has brightly colored outer feathers. They are arranged in simple patterns, and include green, chestnut brown, blue, black, and white. The female, called simply a duck, has dull, plain feathers. She can hide easily when she is incubating her

SOME KINDS OF DUCKS

Common Eider Duck

Mallard

Common Shelduck

Carolina or Wood Duck

Shoveller Duck

eggs or taking care of her young ducklings. In the fall, ducks molt. The drake loses his bright feathers, and turns a brown color like the female. It is sometimes hard to realize that the male and female belong to the same species (*See* POLYMORPHISM.)

After molting, ducks migrate south to winter feeding grounds. They may use the same feeding grounds year after year. The drake and the female duck mate at their winter feeding areas. The new, colored feathers of the drake attract the female. Drakes are territorial, and drive away other males of the same species.

When the ducks migrate to the north during springtime, the male flies with his new mate. Very often, they return to the marsh where she was born. The ducks make a nest on the ground, in places like a clump of grass or a burrow. The female makes the nest. She lays from five to twelve eggs. When she starts to sit on the nest, the drake wanders away and does not help sit on the eggs. The ducklings are hatched in about a month. Most ducklings can run, swim, and find food the day they are hatched. They grow feathers and learn to fly in about five weeks.

Most ducks live in flocks during migration and at winter feeding grounds. You can see them in the fall flying in a ''V'' formation. One or two are at the pointed end of the V, and the rest form two lines trailing on both sides.

Wild ducks are protected by hunting laws and cannot be sold as food. Domestic ducks, the kind the farmer raises, can be sold in markets and are served in restaurants. The most common commercial ducks in the United States are the white Pekin ducks.

P.G.C./M.L.

DUCKWEED (dǝk′ wēd′) Duckweed is a family of 40 perennial aquatic plants that float on ponds in temperate regions. These monocotyledons are the smallest flowering plants known, producing flowers and fruits which are almost microscopic in size. The most common species, *Lemna minor,* has a green, leaflike frond with a tiny root growing into the water. (*See* VESTIGIAL ORGANS.) The frond produces either one stamen or one pistil.

Duckweed plants can double their numbers every 2½ days, and frequently they cover completely a stagnant body of water. Ducks and large goldfish feed on duckweed, helping to keep its growth under control. Duckweed is sometimes grown in home aquariums because it has a mild laxative effect on some tropical fish. Duckweed belongs to the same order as the arum family, and probably descended from the same ancestor as the palm family and the lily family. *See also* PLANT KINGDOM.

A.J.C./M.H.S.

DUCTILITY (dǝk′ til′ ǝ tē) Ductility is the capacity of certain solid substances to undergo permanent changes in shape without breaking. Soft metals, such as copper and gold, can be drawn out into wire finer than a human hair. Such metals are highly ductile. Ductility is a valuable property of many other metals, such as aluminum, iron, nickel, and silver. The term malleability is often used in place of ductility to describe the property of metals that allows them to be hammered into thin sheets.

Some metals are not in the least ductile. Cast iron, for example, fractures quickly when even slightly drawn out to greater length. Cast iron is termed a brittle metal.

Metals are not the only ductile substances. For example, modeling clay is a ductile, nonmetallic substance. J.J.A./A.D.

DUFAY, CHARLES *See* ELECTROSTATICS.

DUNE (dün) A dune is a hill or mound of sand made by the wind. Dunes are found in sandy regions, such as in deserts, along coastlines, and near large bodies of water. A large dune may be 150 to 180 m [500 to 600 ft] high, but most are much lower than that. Dunes usually

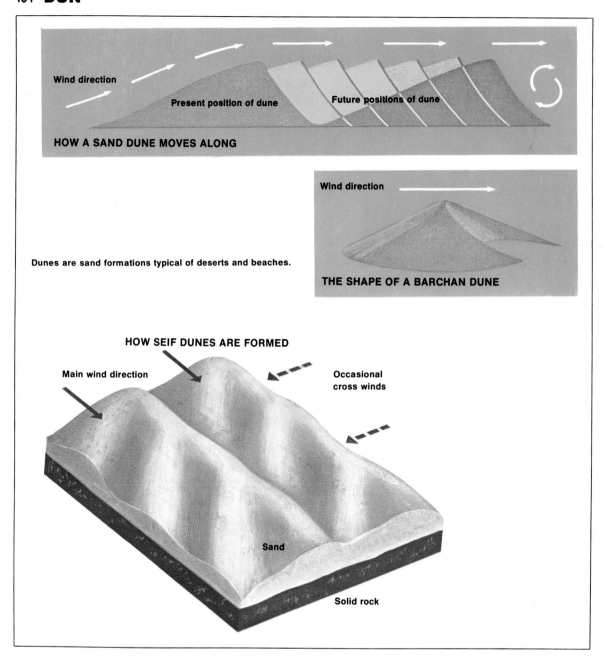

HOW A SAND DUNE MOVES ALONG

Wind direction

Present position of dune

Future positions of dune

Dunes are sand formations typical of deserts and beaches.

Wind direction

THE SHAPE OF A BARCHAN DUNE

HOW SEIF DUNES ARE FORMED

Main wind direction

Occasional cross winds

Sand

Solid rock

have a gentle slope on the side towards the wind, and steep slope on the side away from the wind. Crescent-shaped dunes are called barchan dunes. Seif dunes are long, steep-sided ridges of sand lying in the direction of the main wind movement.

A traveling dune may move across the desert. It loses sand on one side while it gains sand on the other. Some dunes make sounds when the grains of sand are blown by the wind. They are called singing dunes in some parts of the world. Dunes with unusual shapes can be found in Dunes State Park in Indiana. Other areas noted for sand dunes are Cape Cod in Massachusetts, the coastline of the Gulf of California, and the eastern shore of Lake Michigan.

Many ancient Egyptian cities and religious shrines were buried by sand dunes. Grass and trees are often planted to keep dunes from moving into farmlands and inhabited areas. W.R.P./W.R.S.

DUNG BEETLE (dəng′ bēt′ əl) Dung beetles are stocky beetles that use their shovel-shaped heads, broad, spiky legs, and paddlelike antennae to roll animal manure into balls. Each insect then buries its ball, feeding on the manure throughout the summer, and laying eggs early in the fall. The eggs develop into larvae which feed on the manure as they progress through the stages of metamorphosis. Dung beetles perform a valuable service. They help speed along the process of breaking down manure into nitrogen-containing compounds which can be used by other organisms. (*See* FOOD CHAIN; NITROGEN CYCLE.)

Dung beetles are oval, about 2 to 30 mm [.1 to 1.2 in] in length, with short, dark wing covers. In some species the male has an elaborate curved ''horn'' on its head which it uses to overturn other males. A dung beetle is able to consume more than its weight every 24 hours. There are 2,000 species of dung beetles. *See also* SCARAB.   A.J.C./J.R.

DYE (dī) A dye is a chemical compound used to color materials. If properly applied, the shade of a dye is the same throughout the whole fabric.

Dyes are different from paints or stains. Paints and stains do not go much below the surface of a substance. Paint is worn and weathered away. Many stains can be removed with water and soap. A dye must be dissolved before it can work. In this sense, a dye almost becomes part of the fabric itself.

A brief history   People have used dyes to color fabrics and other materials for more than 5,000 years. Dyers have also used mordants for several thousand years. A mordant is a substance used to hold the color to a fabric. Until the 1850s, the range of dyes was limited to a handful of dyes from animal and plant sources.

In 1856, William H. Perkin, a British chemist, made the first synthetic dye, called mauve, which is a pale, bluish purple. His starting material was aniline, then made from coal tar.

Until World War I, Germany was the largest producer of the world's dyes. Since then, the dye industry in the United States has grown rapidly. Today the United States' industries use about 8,000 different synthetic dyes.

Dyeing   Textiles are placed in a dyebath, which is a dye solution. The textile fibers absorb the molecules of the dye. These molecules give the fibers the color. Dyed textiles vary widely in their ability to hold color. But all textiles are somewhat colorfast. Under normal use, a colorfast fabric does not change color. A fabric is lightfast if it does not fade in sunlight. It is washfast if it keeps its color after washing and drying. Some substances, such as chlorine bleach, may affect a fabric's color. (*See* CHLORINE.) Many dyes are not affected by such substances. Mordants are often added to dyebaths to make a substance more colorfast. Mordants combine with the dye molecules. Some chief mordants are tannic acid and soluble compounds of metals such as aluminum, chromium, copper, iron, and tin.

Textiles are dyed in different stages. If the fibers are dyed before being spun into a yarn, the process is called stock dyeing. In yarn dyeing, also called skein dyeing, the fibers are dyed after they are made into a yarn. Most stock and yarn dyeing takes place in large vats.

In piece dyeing, manufacturers apply the dyes after the yarn is made into cloth. Piece dyeing is used for many solid color fabrics. Some dyeing machines pull the cloth through the dyebath. Others operate by squeeze rolls. These rolls force the dye into the cloth.

Types of dyes   The two main kinds of dyes are natural dyes and synthetic dyes. Synthetic dyes have replaced natural dyes in many instances. However, some natural dyes are

These are jet beck dyeing units. They dye fabrics under high pressure, which gives greater color uniformity and also saves water and energy.

still being used. Most natural dyes come from parts of plants, such as bark, berries, leaves, flowers, and roots. The madder plant, grown in Asia and Europe, once supplied bright red dyes for many fabrics, such as silk and linen. Saffron, a yellow dye obtained from the crocus plant, was used to dye silk and wool. Natural indigo, a blue dye, was obtained from the leaves of the indigo plant. Dyers used it on cotton, wool, and other fibers. This dye is still used on denim fabrics. Logwood is a dye which comes from a tree that grows in Central America, Mexico, and the West Indies. Logwood is still used to supply black and brown dyes for cotton, fur, and silk. Henna, an orange brown dye obtained from a shrub of North Africa and the Middle East, was once used to color leather. It is still used in some countries to dye human hair.

There are nine basic kinds of synthetic dyes. Acid dyes are dissolved in acid solutions. These dyes give bright colors to nylon, silk, and wool. Basic dyes are so called because they are dissolved in alkaline solutions. Basic dyes are used on acrylic, wool, and other fibers. Direct dyes color material without the help of a mordant. They are used on cotton and rayon. Premetalized dyes contain metals that improve colorfastness. These dyes are often used on nylon, wool, and acrylic. Disperse dyes dissolve only slightly in water. Dyeing at high temperatures helps dissolve these dye particles into the fibers. Disperse dyes color acetate, acrylic, nylon, and polyester. Reactive dyes form a chemical bond with certain fabrics, including cotton and rayon. Sulfur dyes are dissolved in an alkaline solution. Fibers colored with such dyes are treated with oxygen to help fix the dyes. Vat dyes, processed in a way similar to the sulfur dyes, are among the most colorfast dyes. Sulfur and vat dyes are used chiefly on cotton and rayon.

Dyes contribute greatly to the wide variety of modern clothes and textiles. Dyes are also used by manufacturers in printing designs on fabrics. A machine applies different colors to various areas by means of screens or engraved rolls. This results in different and fascinating arrangements of color in many of the textiles today.   J.J.A./J.M.

DYNAMICS (dī nam′ iks) Dynamics is the branch of physics that is the study of movement. There are three very important laws in dynamics. They are called Newton's laws of motion, after Sir Isaac Newton. He was a very great English physicist who lived 300 years ago. He was the first person to codify these laws.

The first law of motion   An object usually stays where it is. It only moves if a force acts on it. When a body is moving it has a velocity. This velocity will only change if a force acts on the body. Imagine you are pushing a roller along a level piece of ground. If you stop rolling, the roller slows down and stops. This is because of the force of friction that acts between the roller and the ground. So you must keep pushing the roller to keep it moving. You have to push with enough force to overcome the friction force. If you push the roller harder, you increase the force. Therefore its velocity increases.

The second law of motion   When a body speeds up or slows down, it accelerates. Acceleration is the rate of change of velocity. Suppose a body's velocity increases by two meters [6.5 ft] per second, every second. Then its acceleration is two meters per second per second. A force causes a body to accelerate. There is a simple relation between the size of the force acting on a body of constant mass and its acceleration. They are proportional to each other. If the force on a body is doubled, so is its acceleration. The acceleration also depends on the mass of the body. The larger the mass, the smaller the acceleration it will have for a particular force.

An example of this is when you hit a ball. When you do this you are putting a force on the ball. If you hit a ball twice as hard, it will go twice as far. Suppose the ball is twice as heavy. Then you have to hit it twice as hard to make it go the same distance.

The third law of motion   Every force creates a reaction. This reaction is as big as the force. It acts in the opposite direction. When your hand pushes on a table, the table is pushing back against your hand. Your pushing is called the action and the pushing up is the table's reaction. Without this reaction, your hand would push the table down. This does not seem like a law of motion. But it is. Without it, jet planes would not be able to fly. It is the reaction between the hot gases produced by the jet engine and the engine itself, that pushes the aircraft forward.

Moving in a circle   Imagine whirling a stone around on the end of a string. There is a force keeping it moving in a circle. This force

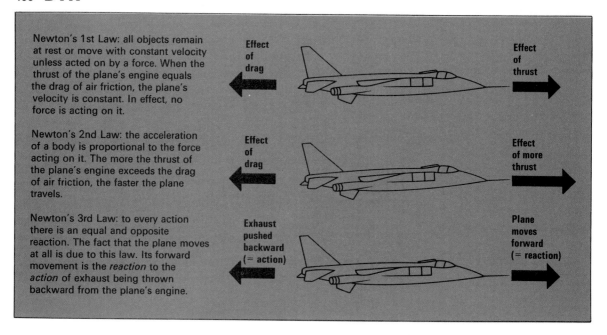

Newton's 1st Law: all objects remain at rest or move with constant velocity unless acted on by a force. When the thrust of the plane's engine equals the drag of air friction, the plane's velocity is constant. In effect, no force is acting on it.

Effect of drag

Effect of thrust

Newton's 2nd Law: the acceleration of a body is proportional to the force acting on it. The more the thrust of the plane's engine exceeds the drag of air friction, the faster the plane travels.

Effect of drag

Effect of more thrust

Newton's 3rd Law: to every action there is an equal and opposite reaction. The fact that the plane moves at all is due to this law. Its forward movement is the *reaction* to the *action* of exhaust being thrown backward from the plane's engine.

Exhaust pushed backward (= action)

Plane moves forward (= reaction)

is the tension in the string. It is the same with a spacecraft orbiting the earth. The force keeping it moving in a circle is gravity. This pull is called the centripetal force. According to Newton's laws of motion, a force produces an acceleration. These objects do not seem to be accelerating, but they are. Their speeds stay the same but the direction of their motion changes. This means that their velocities change. They are, in fact, accelerating. The stone is accelerating towards your hand and the spacecraft is accelerating towards the earth. But this acceleration is balanced by another one. This other acceleration tries to pull them away from the earth or your hand. So they stay as they are, going round in a circle.

Movement and energy   All moving bodies have energy. This energy is called kinetic energy. The amount of it depends on the bodies' velocities and their masses. If a moving ball hits a still one, then the still ball moves. Some of the kinetic energy has been transferred to the still ball. But the total of the energy of motion of the two balls before and after the collision is the same. This is an example of the law of conservation of energy.

In practice, of course, a little of the energy of the moving ball will be lost as friction and in heating up the still ball when they collide. This is because the collision will not be completely elastic—that is, some of the kinetic energy will be absorbed by the balls themselves. There is another quantity that remains the same. It is called the momentum. The momentum of a body is its mass times its velocity. When two balls collide, some of the momentum is transferred. But the total momentum of the two balls remains the same. This is called the law of conservation of momentum.   M.E./J.T.

DYNE (dīn) The dyne is a unit of force in the centimeter-gram-second system. One dyne is equal to the force required to give a mass of one gram an acceleration of one centimeter per second per second.   J.M.C./J.T.

DYSENTERY (dis′ ən ter′ ē) Dysentery is a disease which affects the intestines, particularly the colon. The colon is the part of the large intestine extending from the cecum to the rectum. (*See* INTESTINES.) Dysentery usually includes inflammation of the colon with painful diarrhea. There are frequent movements containing blood and mucus. In some cases, fever and delirium, with a loss of consciousness, may develop. Two varieties of dysentery are amebic dysentery and bacillary dysentery.

A one-celled animal called an ameba causes amebic dysentery. This disease results in harsh inflammation of the colon and bloody diarrhea. Sometimes abscesses, which are swellings consisting of pus, form in the liver or brain. Amebic dysentery is usually spread by taking the amebas on food into the mouth. Fresh vegetables and fruits which have been frequently handled may be infected. The ameba at this time is in a resting, or dormant, stage called the cyst. As the cyst enters the intestines, however, it becomes very active. It grows and reproduces itself. (*See* ASEXUAL REPRODUCTION.) The organism causes the formation of holes, or ulcers, in the bowel. Ulcers may also form in the liver.

Amebic dysentery usually breaks out in warm and tropical countries. But it may also break out in cooler climates. For example, a frightening epidemic of amebic dysentery occurred in Chicago in 1933.

Ways to prevent amebic dysentery involve cleanliness, sanitation, and purification of water. In the treatment of this disease, certain drugs are used, such as emetine. The lack of symptoms does not indicate cure. Treatment should be continued until all amebas are destroyed.

Bacillary dysentery is caused by bacteria. This type of dysentery, quite common during the summer, occurs in all countries and climates. Bacillary dysentery occurs in institutions such as summer camps. The disease spreads by eating foods contaminated with bacteria. The symptoms, similar to amebic dysentery, include harsh, bloody diarrhea, cramps, fever, and loss of appetite. Bacillary dysentery can be prevented by cleanliness, sanitation, and the purification of water and food. Treatment includes a liquid diet and the use of antibiotics.   J.J.A./J.J.F.

DYSPROSIUM (dis pro′ zē əm) Dysprosium is a metallic element. Its chemical symbol is Dy. It has an atomic number of 66 and an atomic weight of 162.5. It melts at about 1,400°C [2,552°F] and boils at about 2,300°C [4,172°F]. Dysprosium is one of the elements called the rare earths. It has seven isotopes. The metal has a valence of three. It forms salts of a yellowish green color. Dysprosium is found naturally in the minerals called gadolinite, fergusonite, euxenite, xenotime, and in other rare earth minerals. It was discovered by the French chemist, de Boisbaudran, in 1886.   D.W./J.R.W.

EAGLE (ē′ gəl) Eagles are large birds of prey found throughout the world except in Antarctica. They have long symbolized power, freedom, and greatness. Among the largest eagles, the bald eagle (*Haliaetus leucocephalus*) and the golden eagle (*Aquila chrysaetos*) grow to a length of 90 cm [36 in], weigh 6 kg [13 lb], and have a wingspan of 2 m [6.6 ft]. As with most birds of prey, the female is larger than the male.

Eagles have large heads, with large, very keen eyes. They have rectangular wings which they use to soar gracefully through the air in search of food. The beak is strong, about 5 cm [2 in] long, the upper part curving over the lower part and ending in a sharp point. The legs and feet are very strong, and the toes end in sharp, clawlike talons. Eagles are aggressive predators, hunting during the day by swooping down on prey, grabbing it and killing it with their talons. Eagles are carnivores and usually eat rodents and small animals, though some eagles prey on larger animals such as chamois, goats, and livestock weighing as much as 10 kg [22 lb].

An eagle usually makes a nest, or aerie, in

The Chinese serpent eagle (facing left) lives in tall forest treetops.

the top of a tall tree. One nest usually serves an eagle for its entire life (20 to 50 years) and may be as deep as 6 m [20 ft] and as wide as 3 m [10 ft]. Eagles begin to mate in the spring of their fourth year and keep the same mates for life. At breeding time, a pair of eagles establishes its territory and prevents all other eagles from entering. (*See* DOMINANCE.) The female lays one or two large eggs 8 cm [3 in] long, weighing 150 g [5.4 oz], and stays with them for 35 to 45 days until they hatch. During this time, the male brings food to the female in the nest. If there are two eggs, the eaglet which hatches first is usually larger, and it kills the other eaglet.

Of the 48 different kinds of eagles, only the bald eagle and the golden eagle are native to North America. Others, such as the serpent eagles, harpy eagles, monkey-eating eagles, and sea eagles, live in widely varied parts of the world. Because eagles sometimes prey on livestock, they are often hunted by ranchers and farmers. Eagles in many parts of the world (including the United States) face extinction from hunting and from poisoning by insecticides and pesticides. Many countries have established laws to protect eagles. *See also* BIRD; CONSERVATION. A.J.C./M.L.

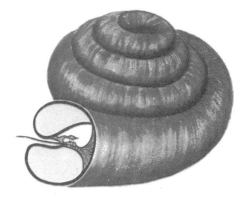

The cochlea, a part of the inner ear, transforms sound vibrations into nerve impulses.

EAR (ir) The ear is the organ of hearing. With our ears, we hear all sound coming from out-side the body. The ear also has a special part that lets us keep our balance. Because we have two ears, we are able to locate sounds in space. We learn to talk by imitating speech sounds reaching us through the ear. Our ears are of primary importance in the process of exchanging ideas and thoughts with other people.

The ear is a complicated and sensitive organ. It changes the vibration of air patterns into electrical signals that reach the brain. It is divided into three parts for the purpose of studying and understanding its action. These parts are the outer ear, the middle ear, and the inner ear.

The outer ear is the fleshy part on the outside of the head. It is called the auricle or pinna. Its main function is to collect sound waves so that they can travel along the external auditory canal to the middle ear. In humans, the pinna lies close to the head, and cannot move around. Certain animals, including the horse, the dog, and the cat, can move their pinnae around to gather sounds more efficiently.

The external auditory canal is about 2.5 cm [1 in] in length, and ends at the tympanic membrane. The tympanic membrane is a thin sheet of tissue about 6 mm [0.25 in] across. Sound waves reaching the tympanic membrane cause it to vibrate, and pass the waves on to the middle ear. The external auditory canal is lined with fine hairs and with very small glands that produce wax. The hairs and wax protect the ear by keeping out dust and small insects.

The middle ear begins with the inner side of the tympanic membrane and ends at another membrane, called the oval window. Within the middle ear are three small bones. The first, called the malleus, is attached to the inner surface of the tympanic membrane. The malleus is then hinged to the incus. Finally, the incus connects to the stapes which is attached to the membrane of the oval window. These three bones, being hinged as they are,

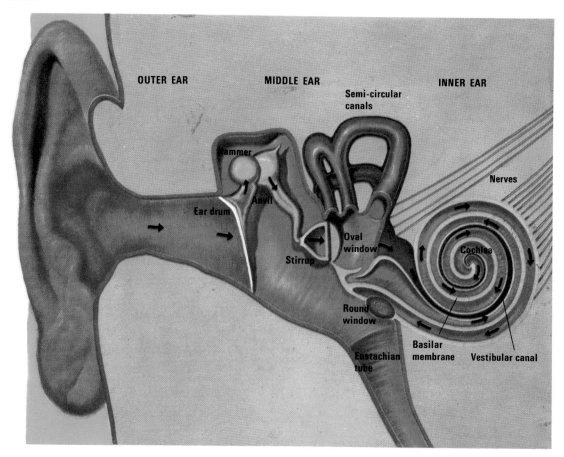

In this cross section, the arrows show the direction of air and mechanical vibrations in the ear.

can move freely and transmit sound waves to the inner ear.

The inner ear contains the cochlea. The cochlea is a cavity in the temporal bone of the skull and has a spiral shape. Sound waves reach the inner ear by vibrations of the oval window membrane. The cochlea is filled with a fluid and a thin length of tissue called the basilar membrane. Attached to this is the sense organ for hearing, the organ of Corti. The organ of Corti contains many tiny hair cells that respond to sound waves. The sound vibrations are changed into nerve impulses which are sent along to the brain through the auditory nerve.

The air pressure on either side of the tympanic membrane must be equalized so that the membrane can vibrate freely. Air can get to the middle ear side of the tympanic membrane through a narrow tube, called the eustachian tube, which is connected with the back of the throat. Hearing can be disturbed if this tube becomes clogged when a person has a cold.

P.G.C./J.J.F.

EARTH

The planet earth (ərth) has developed an ideal environment for supporting life. The oceans, continents, and atmosphere formed over a period of billions of years. Organisms as tiny as bacteria and as large as dinosaurs have evolved, flourished, and died. It is the result of many factors that life as it is known today evolved. (*See* EVOLUTION.)

The earth and the universe The earth is the third planet from the sun. Of the nine

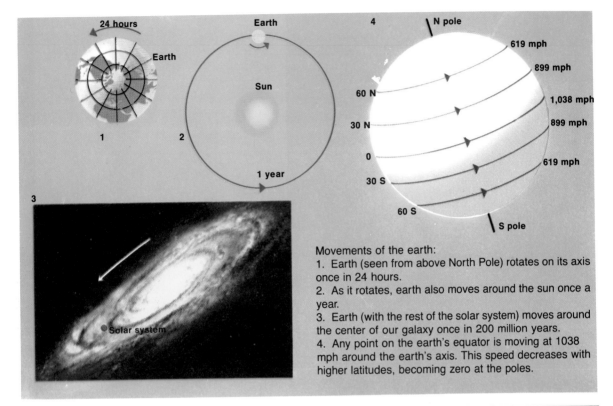

Movements of the earth:
1. Earth (seen from above North Pole) rotates on its axis once in 24 hours.
2. As it rotates, earth also moves around the sun once a year.
3. Earth (with the rest of the solar system) moves around the center of our galaxy once in 200 million years.
4. Any point on the earth's equator is moving at 1038 mph around the earth's axis. This speed decreases with higher latitudes, becoming zero at the poles.

planets, it is the fifth largest. The earth has a diameter of almost 13,000 km [8,000 mi], and a surface area of about 500,000,000 sq km [200,000,000 sq mi]. Water covers about 70% of the surface area.

The earth is always moving in four ways. It spins on its axis, causing day and night. It takes the earth slightly less than one day (24 hours) to make a complete turn. The earth also revolves around the sun, taking about one year for a complete revolution. The axis of the earth also shifts or wobbles like that of a spinning top beginning to slow down. Finally, with the rest of the solar system, the earth swings around the center of the Milky Way galaxy. This trip takes about 200 million years.

The earth spins on an axis which is tilted at 23½° toward a line perpendicular (at a right angle) to its path around the sun. The movement of the earth around the sun and the tilt of the earth's axis cause the seasons.

The nine known planets of the solar system are held to their orbits around the sun by

the force of gravity. Gravity also holds the moon in orbit around the earth. The tides are caused by gravity. The highest tides occur when the earth, the moon, and the sun are in a straight line.

THE EARTH

Diameter: 12,756 km [7,926 mi] at equator

Circumference: 40,074 km [24,901 mi] at equator

Surface temperature:
minimum recorded: −88°C [−127°F]
maximum recorded: 58°C [136°F]

Gases in the Atmosphere:
nitrogen 78.09%
oxygen 20.95%
argon 0.93%
carbon dioxide and others in small quantities

Composition of the Earth's crust:
oxygen 46.60%
silicon 27.72%
aluminum 8.13%
iron 5%
calcium 3.63%
sodium 2.83%
potassium 2.59%
others 1.41%

The earth's crust changes gradually—by erosion, or suddenly and violently, through earthquakes and volcanic eruptions. Mount Etna (above), an active volcano on the coast of Sicily, was photographed at night. The height and crater dimensions of Mount Etna are subject to constant change.

Earth zones   The earth is divided into three main zones: the atmosphere, the hydrosphere, and the lithosphere. The atmosphere is like a gas envelope surrounding the earth. It provides the air necessary for life, and protects the earth from extreme heat and cold. Physical changes in the atmosphere are responsible for the weather. A large percentage of the oxygen in the atmosphere comes from photosynthetic plants. (*See* PHOTOSYNTHESIS.)

The hydrosphere consists of the water and ice on earth. Water is essential for all life on earth. The lithosphere consists of the rocks that form the earth's crust. The three types of rocks found in the earth's crust are classified by how they were formed. They are: igneous rock, metamorphic rock, and sedimentary

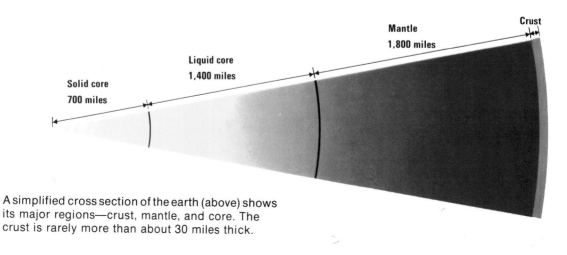

Solid core
700 miles

Liquid core
1,400 miles

Mantle
1,800 miles

Crust

A simplified cross section of the earth (above) shows its major regions—crust, mantle, and core. The crust is rarely more than about 30 miles thick.

The continent of Africa, with the dry Sahara desert in the north, is visible in this photograph of the earth which was taken from space. Such pictures give scientists information about our planet which cannot be obtained on the surface.

rock. The earth's crust varies in thickness from 8 km [5 mi] under the oceans to about 32 km [20 mi] under the continents. Beneath the crust is the mantle, which is about 2,900 km [1,800 mi] thick. Mantle rocks are far more dense than those of the crust. (*See* DENSITY.) Within the mantle is the earth's core. It is thought to be solid at the center, but surrounded by a liquid envelope.

The age and history of the earth   Not long ago, most people believed that the earth was formed recently. Many thought the earth was created in 4004 B.C., a date fixed by generations of people listed in the Bible.

Today, it is generally accepted that the earth formed billions of years ago, possibly from a vast cloud of dust and gases. (*See* COSMOLOGY.)

By studying fossils, scientists have been able to unravel some of the story of life on earth. Methods have been developed that can determine the age of fossils and rocks. (*See* DATING.) Scientists estimate the earth to be about 4.5 billion years old.

The history of the earth is divided into four main time periods: the Precambrian era, the Paleozoic era, the Mesozoic era, and the Cenozoic era. The Precambrian era covers the first 4 billion years of the earth. During this time, the crust of the earth melted and cooled, and many elements were formed. Some primitive organisms lived in the seas about one billion years ago, but before them there are no fossils of living things.

The Paleozoic era began 600 million years ago and lasted about 375 million years. Algae were plentiful, and reptiles, amphibians, and fish became common. Plant life flourished. The Paleozoic era also saw the formation of the Appalachian Mountains.

The Mesozoic era began about 225 million years ago and lasted 160 million years. This was the age of dinosaurs. Cone-bearing plants (conifers) became common, as did insects. Birds and mammals appeared for the first time.

The Cenozoic era started 65 million years ago and extends to the present. During this time, the ice ages occurred. The huge glaciers that moved across the continents had a great effect on the landscape of the earth. Mammals became the dominant land creatures. Flowering plants flourished. The Alps, Himalayas, and Rocky Mountains formed during this period. Perhaps the most important event of the Cenozoic era has been the evolution of humans which occured relatively recently. *See also* ASTRONOMY; GEOLOGICAL TIME SCALE. J.M.C./W.R.S.

An earthquake in 1906 caused great damage (above) in San Francisco.

EARTHQUAKE (ərth′ kwāk′) An earthquake is a movement of the earth's crust that causes the ground to shake or vibrate. Of the thousands of earthquakes that occur each year, only a few are felt or cause major damage. The most destructive earthquakes are those that occur near cities or other populated areas. Most casualties associated with earth-

quakes are caused by buildings or other artificial structures collapsing. However, when an earthquake occurs in a large city, fire is frequently one of the major causes of damage.

Earthquakes are detected by sensitive instruments called seismographs. (*See* SEISMOLOGY.) The strength of an earthquake is measured on the open-end Richter Scale.

Powerful earthquakes may cause huge sea waves called tsunamis. These waves cause heavy damage when they hit the coastline. Fires often spread in an area hit by an earthquake because of broken gas lines and electrical short circuits. For example, in the San Francisco earthquake of 1906, three-fourths of the damage to the city was by fire.

Earthquake zones There are two main earthquake zones: the circum-Pacific belt and the Alpide belt. The circum-Pacific belt, often called the ring of fire, includes the mountain ranges and islands surrounding the Pacific Ocean. The Alpide belt extends across southern Europe and Asia. Other earthquakes occur beneath the oceans along the mid-oceanic ridges.

Cause of earthquakes The earth's crust is made up of about 20 plates that are always moving and rubbing against each other. When the edges of two plates become jammed, tension builds up. The tension is relieved by a sudden movement of the plates, causing an earthquake. Sometimes one plate is forced beneath the other to cause an earthquake.

As tension between two plates builds up, large amounts of energy also build up. When the force finally is released in an earthquake, it is transmitted to the surrounding areas in two waves. The first is the compression, or primary, wave. It acts like a sound wave and creates a rumble or muted boom. This may be people's first warning that a quake is coming.

The secondary, or shear, wave follows. This is the wave that can cause damage. It

This church in southern Italy was almost completely destroyed by an earthquake.

passes through solids of the earth's crust, moving and shaking things at the surface.

The San Andreas fault in western California is thought to be the edge between two plates. In 1906, it shifted, causing the San Francisco earthquake. Seismologists (scientists who study earthquakes) predict that a major earthquake may occur along the San Andreas fault in the next 50 to 100 years.

Other fault lines which could result in earthquakes in the United States are in Hawaii, Missouri, New Jersey, and New England. A series of quakes in 1811-12 in the town of New Madrid, Missouri, may have been the worst in American history. The first quake was felt as far away as Boston, Massachusetts. The series raised about 65 sq km [25 sq mi] of ground 6 m [20 ft]. It caused a new lake to form, and it made the Mississippi River run backwards for a time.

Scientists now generally agree on what causes earthquakes and where they are most likely to occur. When they will happen is still

a matter of continuing research. Accurate forecasts could save many lives.

A number of successful predictions have been made. The most notable was in China in February 1975. Because of the advance warning, officials evacuated people and animals to open ground, and thousands of lives were saved in the severe earthquake which followed.

One of the indicators of the Chinese quake was the strange behavior of animals. Once thought to be merely folk lore, scientists are now studying this aspect of prediction seriously. Many now believe that animals are more sensitive than humans to physical changes that are known to precede a quake. These changes include a shift in the angle or height of ground surfaces, ionization of the air due to the electricity produced by internal pressures, the presence of radon gas, vibrations, shifts in the earth's magnetic field, and the rise or fall of ground water.

With special photographs made from satellites, scientists can measure the actual distance that the earth's crust is moving. From photographs taken at altitudes of 965 km [600 mi], two stations on each side of the San

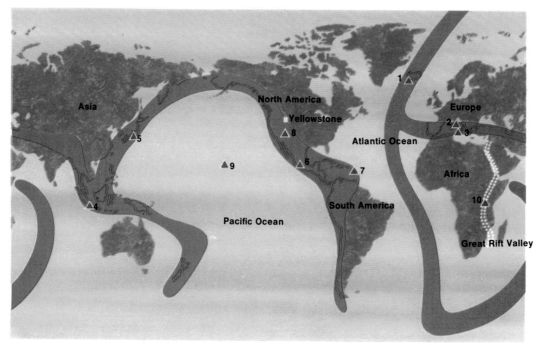

A map (above) of the world's earthquake-prone regions shows that most quakes occur in two great belts of the earth's surface.

Andreas Fault are known to be moving toward each other at the rate of about 9 cm [3.5 in] per year.

Such photographs, and the measure of radon gas released in fault areas, seem to offer the most hope that scientists will be able to forecast quakes with considerable accuracy. *See also* CONTINENTAL DRIFT; PLATE TECTONICS.

J.M.C./W.R.S.

EARTHWORM (ərth′ wərm′) An earthworm is any of 1,800 species of segmented worms belonging to the phylum Annelida. The most common earthworm, *Lumbricus terrestris,* is found in moist soil in temperate regions throughout the world. Earthworms vary in size from 1 mm [0.04 in] to 3.3 m [11 ft]. The earthworm has a very primitive brain, allowing it to respond to heat, light, or touch, but it has no sense organs. Each segment, or annulus, except the first and last, has four pairs of stiff bristles called setae. The setae are made of chitin, and are used for movement.

The earthworm has a complete digestive system. (*See* DIGESTION.) Its alimentary canal runs the entire length of its body with a mouth in the first segment and an anus in the last. As the earthworm moves, it swallows the soil along with any digestible decaying plant matter contained in it. (*See* HUMUS.) Gardeners and farmers consider the earthworm an important animal. As it ''eats'' the soil, it leaves air spaces needed by the roots to grow. The earthworm moves by stretching out its front part, grabbing onto the soil with its setae, then pulling up its rear part. In order to do this, the earthworm has evolved two sets of muscles. Circular muscles surround each segment and can make the worm thinner or fatter. Longitudinal muscles extend the length of the worm and can shorten or lengthen the body.

The earthworm has excretory structures called nephridia in each segment. (*See* EXCRETION.) It has five, heartlike aortic arches that pump hemoglobin-containing blood through two major blood vessels. The earthworm breathes through its skin. Air between particles of soil diffuses across the smooth, moist skin into the blood. (*See* DIFFUSION.) When it rains, these air spaces become filled with water and the earthworm will drown unless it comes to the surface. If the weather is too hot and dry, the earthworm's skin loses some of its moisture, and air cannot diffuse into the worm as easily. This often results in the death of the earthworm.

Earthworms are hermaphrodites, meaning they have both male and female reproductive structures. (*See* REPRODUCTION.) They cannot fertilize themselves, however. (*See* FERTILIZATION.) During mating, the clitellum secretes a mucuslike fluid which surrounds both worms. The clitellum is a swollen band around the worm between segments 32 and 37. After sperm are exchanged, the earthworms move away from each other. A few days later the fertilized eggs are wrapped up in a cocoon produced by the clitellum. Small earthworms emerge from the cocoon within a month. They become sexually mature within three months, and reach full size within a year.

Because earthworms often come to the surface at night when their natural enemies, the birds, are not hunting, they are sometimes called night crawlers. They are also called angleworms because they are often used as bait by fishermen. A.J.C./C.S.H.

EARWIG (ir′ wig) An earwig is any of 1,200 species of insects belonging to the order Dermaptera, and characterized by pincers at the rear of the body. These pincers are used to capture prey, or used for defense, for fighting for a mate, or to help fold up the hindwings. Earwigs also have a pair of thin, membranous hindwings covered by leathery forewings. Some species, however, are wingless or have vestigial wings. (*See* VESTIGIAL ORGANS.)

Earwigs have flat, long, brownish bodies ranging in length from 0.6 to 5.0 cm [0.25 to 2.0 in]. They live in dark, moist places such as in decaying plant matter or under stones. Most species are tropical; there are less than 20 kinds in the United States. These nocturnal insects are omnivores, feeding on both plant and animal matter. Though some earwigs cause damage to fruits and flowers, many also eat pests such as caterpillars, slugs, snails, and thrips.

One worldwide species of earwig is able to defend itself by squirting a foul-smelling liquid from a special gland in the abdomen. Other types of earwigs are parasites on rodents and bats. Earwigs get their name from the superstition that they enter a sleeping person's ear. A.J.C./J.R.

EASTMAN, GEORGE (1854--1932) George Eastman (ēst′ mən) was an American manufacturer and inventor. He made it possible for millions of Americans to become amateur photographers. Early cameras were expensive and bulky, and the developing process was complicated. In 1879, Eastman invented a machine for coating the glass plates used to receive images in cameras. Up to then, the process had been done by hand.

In 1884, he introduced an inexpensive roll film that had a paper base, and a roll holder for winding the film in the camera. The big breakthrough came in 1888. Eastman founded the Eastman Kodak Company in Rochester, New York, and introduced a small, light camera called the Kodak. Kodaks sold for $25, and thousands of people bought them. In 1900, Eastman came out with a $1 model. It sold in the millions, and created a tremendous boom in amateur photography in the United States.

Eastman donated over $100 million to schools and charities. He founded the well-known Eastman School of Music in Rochester. His home in Rochester is now a photography museum. *See also* CAMERA; PHOTOGRAPHY. W.R.P./D.G.F.

EBONY (eb′ ə nē) Ebony is a very hard wood from a tree of the genus *Diospyros*. Ebony trees grow mainly in Japan, the Philippines, India, Sri Lanka, Africa, and North and South America.

The outer wood, called sapwood, is white and often tinged with a gray or pink shade.

The inner wood, called heartwood, is dark brown or black. A hard gum fills the heartwood fibers. This gum probably adds to the property of ebony which makes the wood easy to work and carve. Ebony is used mainly for black piano keys, flutes, knife and brush handles, cabinets, and furniture.

The persimmon trees of the United States and the Orient are a type of ebony. These trees, having very little black heartwood, are of no commercial value. The hard sapwood of the American persimmon is used to make wooden heads for golf clubs.   J.J.A./M.H.S.

ECHIDNA (i kid′ nə) The echidna (*Tachyglossus aculeatus*) is one of only two kinds of primitive, egg-laying mammals or monotremes. (*See* PLATYPUS.) It is native to Australia, New Guinea, and Tasmania. The echidna may reach a length of 78 cm [31 in]. It has a thin, beaklike nose and mouth. Its body is covered with long, dark hair and sharp spines. The echidna has short legs and long, sharp claws which it uses for digging. If threatened, an echidna may roll up in a ball, exposing its spines to an enemy, or it may burrow into the ground for protection.

The echidna feeds at night by digging into ant or termite nests and licking up the insects with its long, sticky tongue. (*See* NOCTURNAL HABIT.) Because of its diet and appearance, the echidna is often called the spiny anteater. The female lays one egg which she keeps in a pouch on her belly. This pouch, similar to that of the marsupials, develops only during the mating season. After the egg hatches, the young echidna stays in the pouch for several weeks, feeding on milk from the mother. Echidnas may live as long as 50 years.
A.J.C./J.J.M.

The echidna (above), or spiny anteater, lives in Australia, New Guinea, and Tasmania. If the echidna is threatened, it may roll up in a ball and expose its spines to its enemy, or it may burrow into the ground for protection.

ECHINODERMATA (i kī′ nə dər′ mət ə) Echinodermata is a phylum of marine animals. They are invertebrates. Included in Echinodermata are the starfish, brittlestar, sea urchin, sand dollar, sea lily, and sea cucumber. They are found in every ocean. Echinoderms live near the shore and at the bottom of the deepest parts of the ocean. They are very abundant. Some stay in one place, others float with the water currents, but most slowly crawl along the ocean floor. Many

Echinoderms shown below (left to right) are: star-fish, sea cucumber, brittle star, and feather star.

move by using small suckerlike projections called tube feet. They feed by filter feeding, picking food particles off the sea floor, or preying on other animals.

Members of Echinodermata have bodies which are round or which have arms and legs growing out in a circular manner. Under a thin layer of skin, they have a chalky skeleton. Echinoderms do not have brains. They breath through gills.   S.R.G./R.J.B.

ECHO (ek′ ō) An echo is a sound that has been reflected (bounced back) from a surface. If a person shouts in a large valley, he usually soon hears the echo of his shout. The sound has reflected from rocks in the valley. The sound takes time to get back to the caller because sound travels in air at a fixed speed. Sound waves travel about 1.6 km [1 mi] in five seconds. A person may hear more than one echo from just one sound. The sound waves bounce from place to place and may produce several echoes.

Sometimes an echo is not heard even though the reflected sound waves reach the ear. The echo may not be heard if the original sound is too weak, or if the reflecting object is too small. It is very difficult to tell the difference between the sound and its echo if the reflecting object is less than 9 m [30 ft] away.

Echoes can help a person find out how far he is away from echo-producing objects. It takes 10 seconds for sound to reach an object 1.6 km [1 mi] away and return. Therefore, a person who wants to find out how wide a canyon is may stand at the edge of the canyon and shout. If he hears the echo five seconds later, he can assume that the canyon is about 0.8 km [0.5 mi] in width.

Sound waves traveling through water also produce echoes. Sonar uses underwater echoes to measure depth and to locate underwater objects. It is used to locate underwater channels and can even detect schools of fish. *See also* RADAR; SONAR; SOUND.   J.J.A./J.T.

ECLIPSE (i klips′) An eclipse occurs when a heavenly body is obscured by a shadow or by another heavenly body. There are two kinds of eclipses visible from the earth: a solar eclipse and a lunar eclipse.

A solar eclipse is an eclipse of the sun. It occurs when the moon moves directly into line between the sun and the earth, so that its shadow falls on the earth. If the sun seems to be covered completely, it is called a total eclipse. During a total eclipse, the day seems to turn to night. It lasts for a maximum of 7 minutes 40 seconds. During a total eclipse, the outer atmosphere of the sun, called the

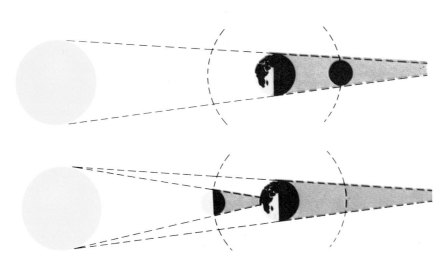

A lunar eclipse (top left) occurs when the earth passes between the moon and sun, casting its shadow over the moon. A solar eclipse (bottom left) occurs when the moon passes between the sun and earth, casting its shadow over part of the earth.

The total solar eclipse of June 30, 1973, seen from a ship off the coast of northwest Africa, is pictured (facing left). A solar eclipse occurs when the moon moves directly into line between the sun and the earth. If the sun seems to be covered completely, it is called a total eclipse.

corona, becomes visible. This aspect of eclipses is of great interest to astronomers.

Not all solar eclipses are total. There is an annular eclipse, where just the middle of the sun is blocked by the moon. In most eclipses, only part of the sun is covered. These are called partial eclipses. Solar eclipses are rare, and only visible from a small area on the earth. Looking directly at a solar eclipse may severely damage the eyes.

A lunar eclipse occurs when the earth is directly between the sun and the moon, so that the moon lies in the shadow of the earth. A lunar eclipse can usually be seen by all people on the night side of the earth. The moon takes on a reddish color during a lunar eclipse because of light being bent by the earth's atmosphere onto the moon.

For thousands of years, eclipses have fascinated as well as confused people. Many people saw solar eclipses as bad omens. Others, like the Babylonians, kept accurate records of eclipses and discovered their regular cycle. See also ASTRONOMY. J.M.C./C.R.

ECLIPTIC (i klip′ tik) The ecliptic is the sun's apparent path through the celestial sphere. The plane of the ecliptic is the plane in which the earth travels in orbit around the sun. Since the moon and the planets are roughly in the same plane, they also follow the ecliptic. See also ASTRONOMY; CELESTIAL SPHERE.

J.M.C./C.R.

ECOLOGY (i käl′ ə jē) Ecology is the study of organisms and their relationship to other organisms and to their surroundings, or environment. It is a branch of biology. A biologist may study a mouse to find out how big it is, what color it is, and how long it lives. An ecologist would study what plants a mouse eats, what animals eat the mouse, and how the numbers of mice affect the numbers of the animals that eat it. The word ecology is frequently misused. People often speak incorrectly of "protecting the ecology of a lake." They should say "protecting the environment of a lake." The environment is the surroundings of a lake. Ecology is the study of those surroundings.

Ecology may be one of the most important sciences. Hundreds of years ago, people did not affect the earth's environment a great deal. Today, modern technology allows us to change many things. We can dig new lakes, drain old ones, build dams, and even remove mountains. Sometimes, when we change things, we accidentally change other things we did not intend to change. In the 1960s, the Egyptians built the huge Aswan dam on the Nile River. The purpose of the dam was to provide water for farmers' fields. It did that, but it also did much more. The extra water behind the dam provided a breeding place for a mosquito that carries the disease bilharzia. Bilharzia is now spreading throughout Eygpt. The dam also stopped rich silt from passing downstream to other fields along the river. These fields are now low in nutrients and no longer yield good crops. (See AGRICULTURE.) In addition, the fish that used to gather at the mouth of the Nile River in the Mediterranean Sea are now gone. All of these things make life harder for the Egyptians.

Ecologists now try to learn more about the environment so they can predict changes before they can occur. In the early 1970s, the United States was planning on building a number of large jet airplanes called Supersonic Transports (SSTs). Ecologists predicted that the jets would damage the environment in the atmosphere. The SSTs were not built.

Ecologists know that people form one small part of a very complicated system on earth. We depend on many things. Many things depend on us. If we are to live successfully on earth, we must learn to live with the natural environment, and to be careful how we change it. *See also* CONSERVATION; POLLUTION.   S.R.G./R.J.B.

ECOSYSTEM (ē′ kō sis′ təm) Ecology refers to the relation of organisms with their environment and other organisms. Ecologists have coined the word *ecosystem* from ecological system. An ecosystem is any naturally occurring unit that includes living and non-living elements which interact to produce a stable system.

An ecosystem can be a very small unit, such as the organisms that inhabit an animal's intestines or those that live on a decaying log. A larger, more complex ecosystem may include all the living and nonliving elements that form a pond or those that form a wooded preserve. The largest ecosystem is called the biosphere, which is the entire portion of earth which holds life. If life is found on other planets, then it would make sense to compare biospheres.

Human beings share the earth with nearly 10 million different species of living things, including plants, animals, insects, and microorganisms. On any area of earth, the populations of plants, animals, and microorganisms make up a biological community. The community is bound together by a complex web of relationships.

Ecologists describe ecosystems by using certain terms. The environment includes such nonliving elements as light, temperature, rain, wind, fire, and soil texture. Chemical processes occur in the environment, including the composition of water in either liquid or gas form, air pollutants, and the composition of soil bearing salt minerals or acids.

Environments may be freshwater, terrestrial, or marine. Some freshwater environments include standing water, such as that found in ponds, lakes, swamps, and bogs. Other freshwater environments consist of running water, such as that found in streams,

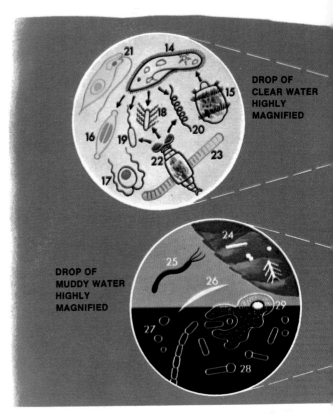

DROP OF CLEAR WATER HIGHLY MAGNIFIED

DROP OF MUDDY WATER HIGHLY MAGNIFIED

Macroscopic (visible to the human eye) pond life in the illustration above includes; (1) duck feeding on underwater plant; (2) hydra feeding on (3) water flea; (4) frog feeding on fly; (5) arrowhead (an aquatic plant); (6) pond snail; (7) duckweed (the smallest aquatic flower); (8) water scorpion and (9) minnow, both feeding on tadpoles; (10) dragonfly; (11) dragonfly larva feeding on (12) small annelid worm; (13) pond skater. These pond life forms make up an ecosystem.

rivers, and springs.

The terrestrial environment is divided into units called biomes. The various biomes include deserts, tundra (treeless plains), alpine meadows, grasslands, savannas (open grassland with scattered shrubs, bushes, and trees), woodlands, evergreen forests, mixed broadleaf and evergreen forests, and tropical rain forests.

The marine environment consists of all seas and oceans. The living parts of a marine ecosystem may include all algae and plants, shellfish, fishes, sea birds, marine mammals,

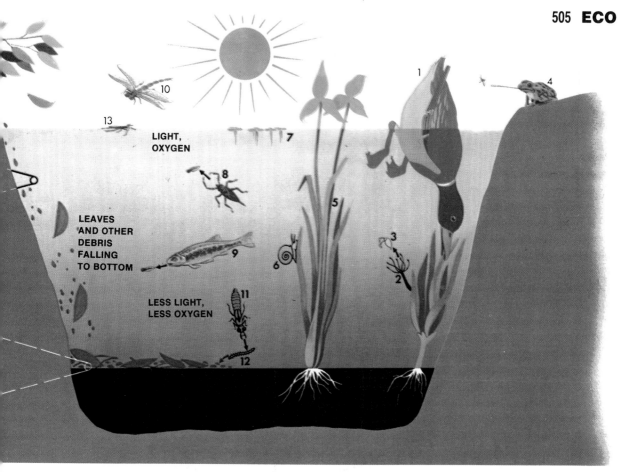

LIGHT,
OXYGEN

LEAVES
AND OTHER
DEBRIS
FALLING
TO BOTTOM

LESS LIGHT,
LESS OXYGEN

A typical pond contains many animals and plants, some microscopic and others macroscopic. The illustration above shows some of these organisms and some of the ways in which they support each other's lives to form a balanced ecosystem. The pond's microscopic life (left) is shown in two magnified drops of water—one from the light, oxygenated water, one from the dark, oxygenless mud.

Microscopic pond life (far left) includes: (14) paramecium being attacked by (15) didinium; (16) diatom; (17) small flagellate; (18 and 19) aerobic bacteria; (20) spirochete; (21) euglena; (22) rotifer; (23) oscillatoria; (24) bacteria feeding on leaf; (25) spirillum, a large bacterium; (26) another diatom; (27 and 28) anaerobic bacteria; (29) amoeba feeding on bacteria and diatoms.

and microorganisms. The nonliving parts may include ocean water, ice floes, ocean floor, rocky coasts, and climate conditions. For a smaller marine ecosystem, an ecologist may consider only plankton, the tiny plants and animals that drift in the ocean and are at the mercy of the currents.

Communities of living things inhabit an environment. The population of a community consists of groups within a single species or several species that live together casually in the same area. For instance, giraffe, zebra, and several antelope species often share the same range on an African savanna. All popu-

lations that occupy a geographic area are called the biotic community.

The habitat is the particular environment in which a population lives. There are many diverse habitats, and some habitats provide a home for tens of thousands of life forms. Cactus plants are found in dry desert areas; catfish live in slow-moving streams and lakes; pronghorn antelope range across the open western grasslands. Each plant or animal population has a certain niche within its community and its ecosystem. Among animal populations, this niche is determined by plant-eating or predator habits.

In each biotic community, an energy flow takes place. Food energy flows from one form of life to another, forming a food chain. When several food chains are interrelated, the energy flow is complex, and the system is called a food web.

Green plants provide the basic food source of all animal populations. The sun is the source of all energy that runs the ecosystem. On land and in the seas, green plants obtain energy from solar radiation in the form of light. Green plants also obtain energy from minerals and nutrients in the soil. In any food chain, green plants are the most efficient producers of food and energy.

Herbivores, or plant-eating animals, are called primary consumers because they eat the green plants. Carnivores, or flesh-eating animals, are called secondary consumers. Deer, rabbits, and mice eat grass, seeds, leaves, and crops, obtaining energy and nutrients directly from plant foods. Bobcats, wolves, and foxes are carnivores. They obtain energy and nutrients by eating the animals that ate the green plants. Plant and animal remains deteriorate because of decomposers such as beetles, earthworms, mushrooms, and various microorganisms. As energy flows through a food chain, it is recycled over and over again and declines.

In understanding the complex interrelationships in an ecosystem, ecologists also study animal habits and behavior patterns, social adaptations, territories, and nesting and feeding sites. If something disrupts the natural order of the system, the entire ecology may be threatened. Plants may not grow well and may not reseed; animals may not breed and reproduce.

Studying ecosystems and resolving conflicts between the different uses of ecosystems can help improve the quality of life and conserve natural environments for future generations. *See also* CONSERVATION; ECOLOGY; ENVIRONMENT; POLLUTION.

D.A.T./G.D.B.

Cactus plants (below) have adapted to the dry habitat of the desert ecosystem.

In contrast with the dry desert ecosystem is the rainforest (above).

ECZEMA (eg′ zə mə) Eczema is a common form of dermatitis, which is a rash or inflammation of the skin. The skin turns red. Fluid-filled pimples, called vesicles, may form. Also, crusts and scales may develop on the surface of the skin. Eczema usually causes the skin to itch. If scratched, the skin may become infected by bacteria.

Doctors believe eczema is caused by an allergy. The allergy results from an extreme reaction to some substances. The substances may be in something the person eats or touches.

Some plants give off certain substances that cause eczema. For instance, oils produced by poison ivy cause a form of eczema when the oils come in contact with a person's skin.

Curing a person with eczema is often very difficult. The most important part in treating eczema is to find out what caused the rash. Doctors test how people react to various substances. This helps doctors find the cause of eczema. Treatment usually involves removing the cause. J.J.A./J.J.F.

EDISON, THOMAS ALVA (1847–1931)
Thomas Alva Edison (ed′ i sən) was one of the greatest inventors in history. He changed the lives of millions of people with inventions such as the electric light, phonograph, and motion picture camera. His concept of inexpensive electricity generated by huge electric power stations made it possible for people to enjoy the benefits of electricity in their homes. Edison patented 1,093 inventions in his lifetime.

He improved the inventions of other people, like the telephone, typewriter, and electric generator. He came close to inventing the radio. Edison predicted the use of atomic energy, and experimented in the field of medicine. He always tried to develop practical devices that would need little maintenance or repair. Edison loved to experiment and was never discouraged by failure. Once, when about 10,000 experiments with a storage battery failed to produce results, a friend tried to console him. ''Why, I have not failed,'' he said. ''I've just found 10,000 ways that won't work.''

Edison had only three months of formal schooling. He was born in Ohio, but spent most of his life in Menlo Park, New Jersey, a suburb of the city of Newark. He became known as the ''Wizard of Menlo Park'' because of his many inventions.

In 1869, Edison made improvements in the stock ticker, an electric device that transmits news of stock prices and displays them on a paper tape. He patented his improvements, and was paid $40,000 for them by the leading manufacturer of stock tickers. That was a large amount of money in 1869. Edison used it to open a workshop and laboratory in Menlo Park.

Edison improved the typewriter in 1874 by substituting metal parts for wood parts. In 1876, he improved the telephone by adding a carbon transmitter. Edison astounded the world in 1877 with his invention of the phonograph, or "talking machine," as it was then called.

In 1879, the inventor worked out the principles for electric lighting. He experimented for two more years to find a filament, or wire, that would give good light when electricity flowed through it. On October 19, 1879, Edison placed a filament of carbonized thread in a bulb. When electricity flowed through the thread it glowed brilliantly, producing a bright light. A short time later, Edison designed one of the world's first electric power generating stations.

Edison developed a motion picture camera in the late 1880s. He experimented with it in a small building near his workshop. The building was called "The Black Mariah" because it was painted black inside and out. Edison made many experimental films inside the "The Black Mariah," including the first boxing match ever filmed. In 1914, he combined the motion picture camera with the phonograph to produce the first "talking pictures." Until then, motion pictures had been silent. The actors' words had been shown on the screen in printed form. Edison's "talking pictures" revolutionized the motion picture industry.

In later years, Edison invented, or improved on, the storage battery, cement mixer, dictaphone, and a duplicating machine. His last patented invention was a method for making artificial rubber from goldenrod plants.

Throughout Edison's life, his work was his greatest joy and companion. He spent long hours every day in his workshop. The inventor received many awards for his achievements. The United States presented him with the Distinguished Service Medal for his de-

sign work on torpedoes in World War I. France awarded him the Legion of Honor. President Dwight D. Eisenhower declared his Menlo Park workshop a national monument in 1956. Henry Ford, the well-known industrialist, once suggested that the period when Edison lived should be called the Age of Edison because of the great inventor's many contributions to mankind.

W.R.P./D.G.F.

EEL (ēl) An eel is a long, snakelike fish that lives in both salt water and fresh water. It is a member of the order Anguilliformes. There are eight families and 55 species of eels in North America. All but the American eel live just in the ocean. Many of these saltwater eels, such as the moray eel, grow large and have many sharp teeth. They can be dangerous to skin divers. The electric eel of South America resembles the true eels in shape. It can produce electricity that can kill or stun other animals. (*See* ELECTRIC FISH.)

The American eel is a member of the family Anguillidae. Adults live in freshwater streams and ponds. When it is time for them to reproduce, they swim down the rivers and travel to the Sargasso Sea, an area in the Atlantic Ocean southwest of Bermuda, where they spawn. (*See* SPAWNING.) The young eels (called elvers) swim to reach the stream in which their parents lived. Males, which grow to 0.6 m [2 ft] in length, do not travel many kilometers up river, but the females, which grow to 1.21 m [4 ft] in length, may ascend the river thousands of kilometers. They even find their way into land-locked ponds and lakes. Eels can travel through underground water passages. This eel migration that goes from fresh water to salt water to spawn is called catadromy. The American eel is the only catadromous fish in North America. Many fishes are anadromous, traveling from salt water to fresh water to spawn. (*See* MIGRATION; SALMON.)

S.R.G./E.C.M.

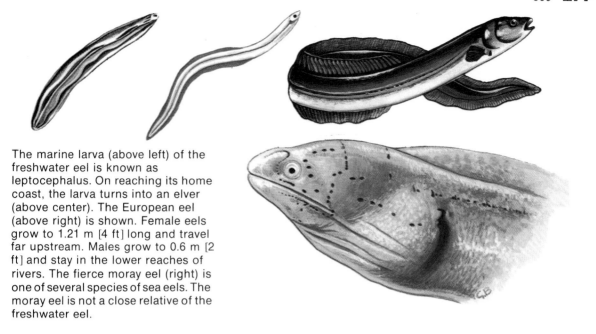

The marine larva (above left) of the freshwater eel is known as leptocephalus. On reaching its home coast, the larva turns into an elver (above center). The European eel (above right) is shown. Female eels grow to 1.21 m [4 ft] long and travel far upstream. Males grow to 0.6 m [2 ft] and stay in the lower reaches of rivers. The fierce moray eel (right) is one of several species of sea eels. The moray eel is not a close relative of the freshwater eel.

EFFERVESCENCE (ef′ ər ves′ əns) Effervescence is the making of small bubbles of gas in a liquid. The gas may be made by a chemical reaction in the liquid.

Effervescence can be seen when adding water to tablets or powders that are meant to calm upset stomachs. The ingredients include weak acids and bicarbonates. They dissolve in the water and react together, producing bubbles of carbon dioxide gas.

Effervescence also occurs when a gas under pressure dissolves in a liquid, and the pressure is then released. This happens, for example, when the cap is removed from a bottle of soda. Carbon dioxide gas dissolved in the soda water leaves the solution and forms bubbles. J.J.A./A.D.

EFFICIENCY (i fish′ ən sē) In physics, efficiency is the amount of energy a machine provides compared to the amount of energy a machine uses. In other words, efficiency is the amount of work we get out of a machine divided by the amount of energy put into the machine. This can be written as a formula or equation.

$$\text{Efficiency} = \frac{\text{output energy or work}}{\text{input energy or work}}$$

Much of the energy put into a machine is lost as heat in overcoming friction. So the efficiency is always less than one. Scientists express efficiency in percentages. For example, the efficiency rating of a four stroke cycle gasoline engine may be as low as 25%. The inefficiency of the engine is due to the high heat loss in the cooling system and the friction in its moving parts.

In all machines, the input energy is never fully converted to output energy. For example, an electric motor may consume 500 watts of electricity to provide 400 watts of useful mechanical power. Power is the rate at which work is done.

$$\text{Efficiency} = \frac{\text{output work}}{\text{input energy}}$$

$$= \frac{400}{500} = 0.8 = 80\%$$

The 100 watts of input power which are not converted to useful output power are converted to heat in the motor. Heat is produced by the electric current passing through the coils or wires in the motor. Heat is also produced by mechanical friction of the motor's moving parts.

The term efficiency is also used in connection with other things besides machines. An electrical transformer can be more than 98% efficient. The human body has an efficiency of about 24%. *See also* ENERGY; MACHINE.

J.J.A./J.T.

EFFLORESCENCE (ef lə res′ əns) Efflorescence is a change that occurs in certain crystals. They become white and powdery when the air is dry. The change occurs because molecules of water evaporate from the crystals. Washing soda is an example of a substance that effloresces. It contains ten molecules of water for each molecule of sodium carbonate. Its formula can be written $Na_2CO_3 \cdot 10 H_2O$. The water in the crystals is called water of crystallization. Up to nine molecules of this water can be lost from each washing soda molecule. This means that the crystals become covered with dry powder when the air is dry. The opposite of efflorescence is called deliquescence. When this happens, crystals take up water from the air around them. D.M.H.W./A.D.

EGGPLANT (eg′ plant′) The eggplant *(Solanum melongena)* is a perennial plant. It produces a large, edible, egg-shaped fruit also called eggplant. The eggplant is a member of the nightshade family and is closely related to the potato. It is native to India and is now grown throughout the world in warm or tropical areas.

The plant is bushlike, growing as tall as 2 m [6.6 ft]. It has large, grayish, prickly leaves, and purple or blue flowers measuring about 5 cm [2 in] in diameter. The fruit reaches a length of 5 to 30 cm [2 to 12 in] and may be purple, brown, yellow, red, white, or striped. The purple variety is the most popular for eating, but it provides few calories or vitamins. A.J.C./F.W.S.

The eggplant (above) is most familiar as a purple fruit. The purple variety is most popular for eating. However, eggplant may be brown, red, yellow, white, or striped. The eggplant is native to India.

EGRET (ē′ grət) The egret is any of several species of long-legged birds belonging to the heron family and characterized by long, elegant feathers called plumes. Egrets usually live in warm areas in or near lakes or marshes, though some species inhabit open grasslands. The egret has a "S" shaped neck, and keeps its head tucked between its shoulders when in flight. The plumes appear only during mating season. They were at one time considered valuable additions to hats and Oriental ceremonial dress. Egrets were once in danger of extinction. Hunters killed millions of them for their plumes and left the helpless young to starve. The Audubon Society and other conservation groups helped establish laws to protect the birds in many areas. (*See* AUDUBON, JOHN JAMES.) There are now protective sanctuaries in South Carolina, Florida, Louisiana, Texas, and in some other states.

The most common egrets in the United States are the great white egret (once called the American egret) and the cattle egret. The great white egret (*Egretta alba*) is about 90 cm [35 in] tall with a wingspan of about 1.8 m [6 ft]. This species produces the longest plumes. The smaller cattle egret (*Ardeola ibis*) stands about 50 cm [20 in] tall with a wingspan of about 1 m [3 ft]. The cattle egret feeds on small insects stirred up by the movement of cattle through open grasslands. Some cattle egrets ride on the backs of the cattle and water buffalo. They pick ticks and other insects from the animal's skin. (*See* SYMBIOSIS.) Cattle egrets came to South America from Africa about 50 years ago and only reached the United States after World War II (1945).   A.J.C./L.L.S.

EHRLICH, PAUL (1854–1915) Paul Ehrlich (ār′ lik), a German bacteriologist, became known for discovering the drug arsphenamine, also called Salvarsan. Salvarsan was the first effective treatment for syphilis. Ehrlich believed that, since certain dyes stick to certain living tissues and stain them, it ought to be possible to find a poisonous dye that could stick to germs and kill them. In 1910, after many tests, Salvarsan was found suitable for this purpose. Salvarsan is also called ''606'' because it was the 606th compound tested.

Ehrlich also did much work on the use of dyes for studying living tissues, and on the bacteria that cause tuberculosis. He also worked on increasing immunity to disease. He developed a diphtheria antitoxin. In 1908, for his work on immunity, Ehrlich shared the Nobel Prize for Medicine with Elie Metchnikoff.   J.J.A./D.G.F.

EIDER (īd′ ər) The eider is a sea duck that belongs to the family Anatidae. It is a heavy-bodied duck with a short neck and wings. There are four species of eiders in North America. Two species are found mainly in Alaska. The other two species live throughout the northern part of the continent. The feathers from these ducks were once commonly used as stuffing for pillows, mattresses, sleeping bags, and clothing. They are very light but hold warmth well. *See also* DUCK.   S.R.G./L.L.S.

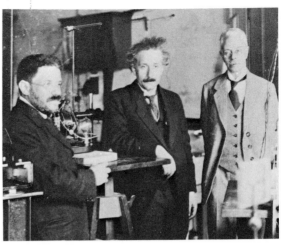

Albert Einstein, one of the great pioneers of modern physics, is pictured in the center.

EINSTEIN, ALBERT (1879–1955) Albert Einstein (īn′ shtīn), a German-American scientist, was one of the greatest contributors to modern physics. Einstein was born in Ulm, Germany, but soon moved to Munich. After public school in Munich and in Aarau, Switzerland, Einstein studied math and physics at the Swiss Polytechnic Institute in Zurich. He was graduated in 1900. He became a Swiss citizen at the age of 22. From 1902 to 1909, he was employed at the patent office in Berne, Switzerland. During these years, Einstein published the first part of his famous theory of relativity. In 1914, he became a professor at the Prussian Academy of Science in Berlin, Germany. In 1921, Einstein received the Nobel Prize for physics. In 1932, Princeton University offered Einstein a lifetime professorship. He accepted the offer, providing he could divide his time between Princeton and the Prussian Academy of Sciences. Conditions in Germany in 1933 made it very difficult for Jewish people to live there. In 1940, Einstein became a United States citizen.

Einstein's ideas   Einstein's theory of relativity greatly changed scientific thought with new concepts of time, space, motion, and gravitation. His formula, $E = mc^2$ is one of the most important equations in science. In this formula, E stands for energy, m for mass, and c^2 for the speed of light multiplied by itself. This formula shows that matter, which is any material or substance, if completely changed to energy such as heat or light, would produce a huge amount of energy.

With the knowledge of this formula, it became possible to imagine the atomic bomb and later to make it.

Many of Einstein's ideas were difficult to understand. Some of them, however, came out of other quite basic ideas. For example, to a person living in New York, Pittsburgh is west. To a person living in Arizona, Pittsburgh is east. The direction of Pittsburgh is relative. It depends on where a person is. The same kind of idea is true for things that move. For example, if a person is sitting in a train, and another train begins to pass by the window, it is puzzling for the person to tell which train is moving. Therefore, motion is relative. Einstein built on these ideas. He included the motion of light itself in his thinking. He joined together space and time in a new theory of relativity. (*See* RELATIVITY.)

Einstein also made great advances in the quantum theory. He suggested that light could be thought of as a stream of tiny particles called quanta. Using his theory of quanta, Einstein explained the photoelectric effect. He showed that when quanta of light energy strike atoms in certain metals, the quanta force the atoms in the metal to release electrons.

Einstein also studied the Brownian movement, an irregular motion of tiny particles suspended in a liquid or gas. This movement showed that atoms and molecules are always in motion.

Einstein was also concerned with the force of gravity and electromagnetism. Einstein believed that gravitation is not caused by some mysterious force in matter. He thought that gravitation is caused by inertia itself. Inertia means that a body cannot by itself change its state of rest or motion. Unless some outside force affects an object, the object con-tinues to rest or move as it was moving. Einstein also thought that the inertia of a body forces it to take a certain path through a space, which would bend when it came near a large mass of matter, such as the sun.

Einstein tried to combine electromagnetism and gravitational force in a single theory called unified field theory. Einstein failed to establish such a theory. He spent the last 25 years of his life working on it.

J.J.A./D.G.F.

EINSTEINIUM (īn stī′ nē əm) Einsteinium is a radioactive element. The chemical symbol for einsteinium is Es, and its atomic number is 99. It has an isotope, Es-254, with a half-line of 270 days. It is named for the great physicist Albert Einstein. It does not occur naturally. It was first detected after a hydrogen bomb explosion in 1952, having been formed during the explosion. It is produced by nuclear bombardment of certain heavy elements.

D.W./J.R.W.

The eland, found in southeast Africa, is the tallest and heaviest of the antelopes.

ELAND (ē′ lənd) The eland is the largest of the antelopes, standing 1.8 m [6 ft] tall at the shoulder and weighing as much as 950 kg [2090 lb]. It has spirally twisted horns, about 1 m [3.3 ft] long, humped shoulders, and a dewlap (flap of skin) hanging from the neck.

The eland usually has 8 to 15 vertical stripes on its sides and a black stripe along its back. This mammal is native to Africa and grazes in herds of 200 or more in open plains and light forests. The eland is a valuable farm animal. It is easily trained, has an immunity to many local diseases, and can go for weeks without water.

There are two major species of elands. The common eland (*Taurotragus oryx*) is pale brown in color and lives in southern Africa. The larger Derby eland (*Taurotragus derbianus*) is reddish brown, has heavier horns, and lives in central Africa.   A.J.C./J.J.M.

ELASTICITY (i las′ tis′ ət ē) If an object is stretched and let go, two things can happen. It can stay stretched or it can return to its original shape. If it springs back, it is said to have elasticity. Rubber and steel are both elastic materials.

An object is stretched by applying a force. For an elastic object, the amount it stretches is proportional to the force. For example, if the force is doubled the object is stretched through twice the distance. This is called Hooke's law. It was first discovered by Robert Hooke, an English physicist.

An elastic body can only be stretched a certain distance. If more force is applied to it, two things can happen. It can break or it can stay stretched at the same distance. When this happens it has passed its elastic limit. If it is stretched still more, the yield point is reached. Then only a small extra force stretches it a lot. Narrow necks start to appear. Eventually one of the necks gets so narrow that it breaks.

When an object is stretched, it is said to be under stress. There are other ways of stressing an object. One way is by twisting it. This is called torsion. Only elastic materials return to their original shape when twisted and then let go. Non-elastic materials stay twisted. Hooke's law also applies to this type of stress. In this case, you measure the angle that the object is twisted through. For an elastic object, this angle is proportional to the twisting force. Again there is an elastic limit. If the object is twisted too far, it will remain twisted.

There are other important types of stress. One is called the shear stress. This stress is like pushing along the top of a deck of cards. When you do this, the deck deforms and the cards spread out. With a shear stress, objects deform and spread in the same way. Another kind of stress is when you squash an object on all sides. This happens to objects at the bottom of the sea. Hooke's law applies to both these stresses.

A golf ball (above) goes out of shape when hit by a club. Because the ball is made of very elastic materials, it resumes its original spherical shape as soon as it leaves the club.

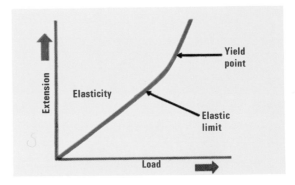

A graph (above) plots the extension of a body against the force acting on it, and a straight line occurs. The body loses elasticity past its elastic limit and stretches past the yield point.

All solids are made up of atoms. The atoms are held together by bonds. The bonds are like springs. When an object is stressed, the atoms are pulled apart. This means that the bonds are stretched. When the stress is released, the atoms spring back. All solids have weak points, such as a crack on the surface. The bonds at these points break more easily than others. When an object is stretched, these are the first bonds to break. This happens to brittle objects such as porcelain.

Rubber is a very elastic material. It stretches very easily. It does this because of its atoms. They are arranged in long molecules. (*See* MOLECULE.) These molecules are coiled. When rubber is stretched, the molecules uncoil. Only a small force is needed to uncoil the molecules. M.E./J.T.

ELASTIN (i las′ tən) Elastin is a protein found in the elastic fibers and elastic tissues of an animal's body. It is made of a large molecule which can coil or uncoil to give elastin its elastic properties. (*See* ELASTICITY.) Elastin makes up the yellow, branching elastic fibers found in connective tissue. Elastin is also part of the elastic tissues in the fat of an animal's body. A.J.C./E.R.L.

ELDERBERRY (el′ dər ber′ ē) The elderberry is a small black or red berry produced by the elder plant. The elder plant is any of 40 species of trees or shrubs belonging to the honeysuckle family and growing in temperate regions throughout the world. The elder plant grows as tall as 75 cm [30 in] and has leaves divided into five pointed and toothed leaflets. There are large clusters of small, white, saucer-shaped flowers which are followed by small fruits called elderberries. Elderberries are a food source for wildlife. They can also be processed into medicines or wine. A.J.C./M.H.S.

ELECTRIC BELL (i lek′ trik bel′) The doorbell in the average home is an electric bell that works on a principle of electromagnetism. A piece of iron can be made magnetic when an electric current is passed through a coil of wire wrapped around it. The iron and the coil form an electromagnet.

In the electric bell, a piece of iron, called an armature, is drawn toward the ends of a U-shaped piece of iron when the U-shaped piece is magnetized. The electric current also passes through the armature to a contact. When the bell is not being rung, the armature is held against this contact by a spring. The pressing of a button starts the current flowing from a battery. The armature is pulled away from the contact. At the same time, a hammer attached to the armature strikes a bell. However, separating the armature from the contact stops the electric current, and therefore the magnetism of the U-shaped piece of iron. The armature is then drawn back to the contact by the spring. This order of events is repeated as long as the button remains pressed producing the rapid ringing sound of the bell. J.J.A./J.T.

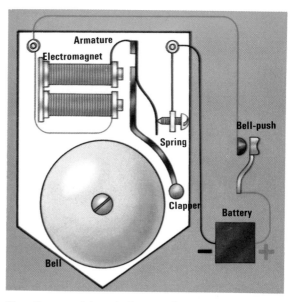

The diagram (above) shows a battery-powered house door-bell, a common type of electric bell.

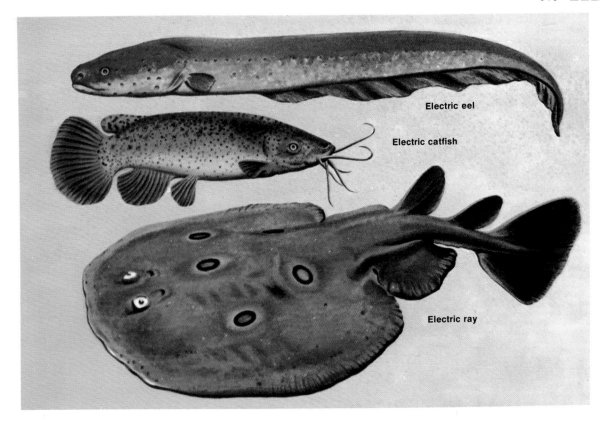

Electric eel

Electric catfish

Electric ray

The best-known electric fish are the electric eel (which produces shocks of up to 550 volts), the electric catfish, and the electric ray.

ELECTRIC FISH (i lek′ trik fish) A number of species of fishes are able to produce electricity in their bodies. The better-known electric fishes are the electric eel, the electric catfish, and the electric ray. (*See* CAT-FISH; EEL; RAY.) They produce electricity with special muscles. Most muscles contract when a nerve stimulates them. A special ''electric'' muscle cannot contract. When a nerve stimulates it, an electrical shock is produced. The electric eel is able to produce a discharge up to 550 volts. This is enough to stun a large animal that is standing in the water.

Electric fishes usually use the electricity to defend themselves. Some of the fishes use it to stun and capture prey. The electrical field is also used by fish to find their way in muddy water, similar to the way radar is used.

S.R.G./E.C.M.

ELECTRICITY

Electricity (i lek′ tris′ ət ē) is a property of nature that we usually know as electric current. We cannot see it, but we can see its effects. Rubbing two things together sometimes produces electricity. This happens when you take off a nylon sweater. The nylon rubs against your hair or your clothing. The electricity causes crackling and sparks. This effect has been known for thousands of years. A Greek philosopher called Thales noticed it in 600 B.C. He rubbed a piece of amber. When he did this, the amber tried to pull things towards it. This is because it had an electric charge. This is how electricity got its name. It comes from the Greek for amber, *elektron*.

Another effect of electricity is lightning. This was not always known. The American scientist Benjamin Franklin first showed this

connection between electricity and lightning.

In 1780, another effect of electricity was noticed. An Italian named Luigi Galvani touched the back leg of a dead frog with his knife. When he did this, the leg twitched. He guessed that this was due to electricity. Another Italian, Count Alessandro Volta, found out what was happening. The knife was made out of brass and iron. These metals acted on a certain liquid in the frog's leg. This produced electricity and led to the discovery of the voltaic cell and the battery. (*See* BATTERY.) They were both invented in 1800.

Soon afterward, scientists started to study electrochemistry. In the 1830s, the English scientist Michael Faraday discovered the laws of electrolysis. By this time electric circuits were being built. In a circuit, an electric field is established in a wire, and it is possible that a current travels along a wire. In 1831, Faraday made a great discovery. He took a circuit that did not have any current running through it. Then he moved it around inside a magnetic field. This produced a current in the circuit. Faraday had discovered a very good way of producing electricity. This method is still used today in generators. Generators produce electricity for homes and factories. Faraday also discovered the opposite effect. He placed a wire with a current running through it between the poles of a magnet. When the current changed, the wire moved. This effect is now used in electric motors. The links between electricity and magnetism are studied in electromagnetism.

Soon large generators were being built. Electricity was beginning to come into use in the United States and Europe. Industry began to use electric motors to replace some steam engines.

New inventions   Many new inventions were made. An American inventor named Thomas

The tower of the wind turbine (facing left) is 60 m [200 ft] high, and the blades are 91 m [300 ft] from tip to tip. The turbine can generate 2.5 megawatts of electricity.

Electricity in nature is typified by lightning—the flashing of light produced by a release of atmospheric electricity from a cloud.

The electric light bulb typifies the harnessing of electricity. The first light bulb was made by Thomas Edison in 1879.

Edison made an important discovery. When a current passes through a wire, the wire is heated. Edison found a way of making the wire become so hot that it glowed. This effect is now used in the electric light and the electric heater which provide light and heat in millions of homes throughout the world.

In 1837, the telegraph was invented by two English scientists, Sir Charles Wheatstone and W. F. Cooke. Samuel F. B. Morse also worked on the telegraph in the United States. Morse invented the relay. This device allowed telegraph messages to be sent over long distances. In 1851, the first telegraph cable under the sea was laid. It linked Britain and France. In 1866, a cable was laid under the Atlantic Ocean. It linked the United States and Britain. Then, in 1875, Alexander Graham Bell invented the telephone.

Another discovery concerned with electricity was that of radio waves. In 1864, James Clerk Maxwell proved with mathematics that radio waves should exist. In 1887, they were detected by Heinrich Hertz. The first person to think of using them for communicating was Guglielmo Marconi. He sent his first radio message across the Atlantic Ocean in 1901.

Radio broadcasting did not start until after World War I. Before broadcasting could start, amplifiers had to be invented. In 1907, Lee de Forest invented the triode vacuum tube. This tube can be used for amplifying. A few years later, engineers realized this and soon broadcasting began.

Another very important invention was the cathode-ray tube. These tubes are used in television sets. Before television could be invented, there were many complicated problems to be solved. It was finally invented in 1926 by John Logie Baird in Britain.

During World War II, electronics made great advances. New inventions meant that radar could be used. Radar also uses cathode-ray tubes. Since then, many new electrical machines have been built. Electricity is used in washing machines, dishwashers, trains, and many other kinds of machines.

What is electricity? When scientists discovered electricity, they thought it was a fluid like water. They thought there were two kinds of electricity, one positive and one negative. They thought that electricity was made up of two fluids. That is why they used the term electric current. They also talked about resistance. A high resistance slows down the flow of the fluid. We still use these words today, though we no longer think of electricity as a fluid. Around the 1830s, scientists began to think that electricity might consist of particles. This idea became more and more popular. It was not until 1897 that these particles were discovered by Sir J. J. Thomson. They were called electrons. The electron is a very small particle with a very small electric charge. A typical flashlight bulb uses a current of one ampere. A circuit of one ampere has six billion billion electrons flowing around it every second.

There are several different quantities in electricity. Many different instruments are needed for measuring them. These quantities are measured in different units which are often named for famous scientists. The amount of electric charge is measured in coulombs. This is named for the French physicist, Charles Coulomb. Current is measured in amperes. André Ampère was a French scientist who studied electricity around 1800. The resistance of a material is measured in ohms, after Georg Ohm. (*See* OHM'S LAW.) Potential and electromotive force are measured in volts, after the Italian scientist, Alessandro Volta.　　M.E./A.I.

ELECTRICITY SUPPLY (i lek′ tris′ ət ē sə plī′) Electricity is the most important form of power that we have. We use it for heating and lighting in the home. We use electricity for cooking. We use it for TV and radio. We use it in industry to drive hundreds of different

A man (above) is performing maintenance work on a huge electricity generator in a power station. Steam produced by coal, oil, or nuclear energy drives the turbines which power these generators. There are several different kinds of electricity generating stations.

kinds of machinery. It has been estimated that a worker in industry has the equivalent of over 500 slaves working for him because of the electric power that he can use. It is very hard to imagine a world without electricity. For everybody in the country to receive a supply of electricity, huge generating stations are needed. There must also be a network of power supply lines. The power lines that cover the country are called the electricity grid.

Generating stations Most electricity is produced by generating stations that supply

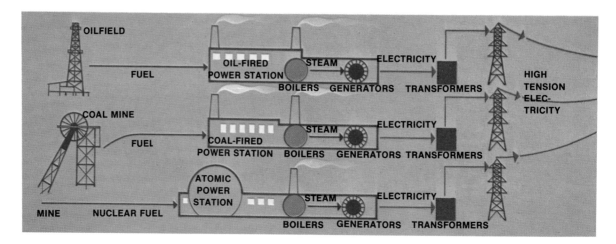

The diagram (above) shows in schematized form how electricity is distributed from power stations to industrial users and ordinary homes. Before the electricity goes into individual homes, transformers at local power stations turn the high voltage electricity into low voltage electricity.

Huge transformers (above) in power stations increase the voltage of electricity.

power to wide areas of the country. Some big industries have their own generating stations. This means that they do not have to rely on the public supply. The first electric supply stations were set up in 1882. They were designed by Thomas Edison. He built one in London, England, and two in the United States. These stations supplied direct current to only a few dozen users. In 1886, George Westinghouse built supply stations that produced alternating electric current. Alternating electric current (AC) is safer and more convenient than direct current (DC).

Electricity generating stations are of several different kinds. Some use the energy that comes from water stored behind dams. These are hydroelectric stations. Some generating stations burn oil or coal to heat water and make steam. The steam is then used to turn big turbines. The turbines generate the electricity. Modern generating stations are also designed to use atomic fuel. These are the nuclear or atomic stations.

When the electricity has been produced, it must be distributed. To distribute the electricity, transformers are first used. A transformer increases the voltage of the electricity. The cables that carry electricity in the grid carry it at very high voltage. The voltage of electricity produced by a generator is only a few thousand volts. With the help of a transformer, this becomes many thousands of

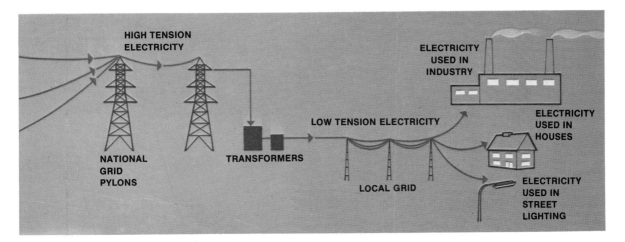

volts. Sometimes hundreds of thousands of volts are used in the power lines. Such a large voltage is used because less power is lost in the cables.

Power lines About half a million miles of power lines are used to supply electricity across the United States. This is long enough to stretch to the moon and back again. The power lines are high-voltage lines. Most users of electricity do not need it at very high voltage. The electricity used by most people is only at about 120 or 200 volts. To turn the high voltage electricity into low voltage, transformers are again used. The transformers are in local power stations. From the local power stations, the electricity is distributed to houses and factories nearby, and to the streets for lighting.

Electricity power lines are made of copper or aluminum. They are insulated. The insulation must be very strong. It is usually plastic or oiled paper, in many layers. In the open country, the supply lines are hung from tall pylons, or towerlike structures. The lines of pylons stretch for miles. In the city, it is often too dangerous to have electric cables hanging overhead. Instead the cables are buried in the ground. Laying cables underground is very expensive. They cost more than building pylon lines and overhead cables. *See also* GENERATOR, ELECTRICAL.   D.W./A.I.

ELECTRIC LIGHT (i lek′ trik līt′) Electricity can be used to produce light in three ways. It can be passed through a wire so that the wire glows red hot or white hot. Electricity can be made to pass through a gas. This makes the gas glow and give off light. It can be passed through special substances that glow when an electric voltage is applied to them.

Light has been produced by passing electricity through wires for over a hundred years. In 1859, Moses Farmer lit his house in Salem, Massachusetts with electric lamps he had invented. The wires in the lamps were made of platinum. The wire that glows in a lamp is called a filament. The inventor Thomas Edison found that better light was produced if the filament were made of carbon. However, such lamps were more difficult to make. They had to have most of the air inside them taken away. Unless the air were removed, the carbon burned when it became hot enough to glow.

Today, the filaments of lamps are often made of the metal tungsten. Tungsten gives a much whiter light than carbon when it glows. The filament is made in a coil shape. The bulb contains the gases nitrogen and argon. These do not react with the metal of the filament. The metal does not burn or evaporate. Most light bulbs in the home use between 40 and 150 watts of electric power. In TV studios and

In the office (above) the entire ceiling has subdued electric lighting, which avoids glare and gives an effect as much like daylight as possible.

in searchlights, there are large tungsten lights that use as much as 30,000 watts.

Many of the lights that are used for street lighting and for business signs are tubes containing gas. When electricity is passed through the gas, the energy makes the atoms of gas glow brightly. Different gases and vapors glow in different colors. Neon glows bright red. Sodium vapor glows yellow. Mercury vapor gives a bluish white light. These lamps are called discharge lamps.

Arc lamps give very bright light. Electricity is made to jump from one electrode to another through the air. In a carbon arc light, the electrodes are rods of carbon. Carbon arc lights are sometimes used for motion picture projectors. They also make very good searchlights.

Another kind of lamp that contains a gas is called a fluorescent lamp. (*See* FLUORESCENCE.) A fluorescent lamp contains mercury vapor. When an electric current is passed through mercury vapor, it produces bluish white light. It also produces invisible rays. These are called ultraviolet rays. The lamp has a special layer of powder inside its glass. The powder is called a phosphor. When a phosphor is struck by ultraviolet rays, it glows. The light it gives off may be white or any of several different colors. Zinc silicate is a phosphor that gives off green light. Calcium

tungstate gives off blue light. Magnesium tungstate produces yellowish white light.

Flat panels of glass can also be used as sources of light. Instead of sticking the phosphor inside the fluorescent tube, it is stuck to the glass like a sandwich between two electrodes. Zinc sulphide is a phosphor that glows when an electric current flows through it.

D.W./J.T.

This French train is powered by electricity.

ELECTRIC MOTOR (i lek′ trik mōt′ ər) An electric motor is a kind of machine. It is a machine that uses the energy of electricity to do work. Electric motors mostly use electrical energy to make wheels turn. A motor that makes wheels and shafts turn is called a rotary machine. There are very many ways in which wheels and shafts turning around can be made to do work for us. Washing machines, vacuum cleaners, drills, and fans all rely on turning parts to do their job. Electric pumps have blades that spin at high speed to push liquids or gases along tubes.

Electric railroad trains and electric automobiles have shafts, gears, and driving wheels that are turned by electric motors. Not all electric motors turn wheels, however. There are modern electric motors that can move loads along tracks without wheels. The tracks must be specially built. Motors like this are called linear induction motors.

Electric motors depend upon electromag-

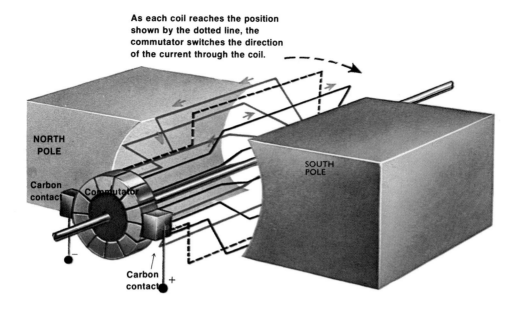

As each coil reaches the position shown by the dotted line, the commutator switches the direction of the current through the coil.

NORTH POLE

SOUTH POLE

Carbon contact

Commutator

Carbon contact

A diagram of a many-coiled DC (direct current) electric motor is shown above. The coils form the armature, which is pivoted on a drive shaft between the north (N) and south (S) poles of a fixed magnet. When current passes through the armature (as shown by arrows) each coil becomes magnetized, and rotates until its N pole is next to the S pole of the fixed magnet. At this point, the commutator switches the direction of the current. The N pole of the coil becomes a S pole and is repelled by the S pole of the fixed magnet, so that rotation continues. A one-coil motor does not run smoothly, because the magnetic force that rotates it varies with the relative positions of the coil and magnet. It also jerks when the commutator switches the current.

netism. Whenever an electric current flows in a wire, the wire acts like a magnet. If the wire is bent into a loop, one side of the loop acts like a north pole and the other side like a south pole. If the wire is bent into many loops, this forms a coil. The coil becomes strongly magnetic. Now it moves just like one magnet does when it comes near to another. The north pole of a magnet is attracted by the south pole of another magnet. It is pushed away, or repelled, by another north pole.

An electric motor has two main parts. One part is fixed. This part is called the stator. Inside the stator is a part that can turn. This is called the rotor, or armature. The rotor consists of coils of wire. They are wound around pieces of soft iron, called cores. The iron increases the strength of the magnetism when electricity passes through the coils. The stator in simple motors is a permanent magnet. (*See* MAGNETISM.) In other motors it is made of coils of wire, like the rotor. Coils like this are called a field winding.

There are two main kinds of electric motor. One kind uses direct current electricity, or DC. The other uses alternating current, or AC. In a DC motor, the coils of the armature are fed with electric current through pieces of carbon on each side. The pieces of carbon are called brushes. The brushes touch a ring of metal pieces fixed around the shaft of the armature. This ring is called the commutator. Electric current flows from one carbon brush, through the commutator, into the coils of the armature. From the armature, it flows out again through the commutator into the other carbon brush.

As soon as electricity flows through the armature coils, it makes the armature into a magnet. The north pole of the armature is attracted by the south pole of the stator. The south pole of the armature is also attracted by the north pole of the stator. This makes the armature turn. The shaft of the motor turns round as the armature turns.

When the armature turns to a certain point, it might be expected to stop. Its north pole must reach a point as close as it can reach to the south pole of the stator. But the armature is turning very quickly. It moves past that point, because of its momentum. Now the electric current passing through the armature changes direction. It does this because the commutator has turned as well. Different pieces of metal in the ring are in contact with the carbon brushes. The electricity in the coils of the armature flows in the other direction.

The north pole of the armature turns into a south pole. As soon as it does this it is pushed away from the south pole of the stator. Now it is the north pole that attracts it. So the armature keeps on turning. In most electric motors, there are several separate coils in the armature. It acts like a magnet with many different north and south poles. The poles change continually as the armature spins and makes the commutator change the direction of the current. The more separate coils there are, the more smoothly the motor turns.

Electric motors that use AC work in a different way. In one kind, the alternating current is passed around coils in the stator. The result is a moving magnetic field. When there is a moving magnetic field, it causes current to flow in wires nearby. This is called induction. Induction makes an electric current flow in the coils of the armature. This makes the coils behave like magnets. The moving magnetic field of the stator makes the coils of the armature spin. The armature turns the shaft of the motor. This kind of electric motor is called an induction motor.

Another type of electric motor that uses alternating current is called the synchronous motor. In this type the rotor spins at the same speed as the turning magnetic field of the stator. Electric clocks usually have synchronous motors. They have to have a constant

speed of rotation. Synchronous motors are also used in other scientific instruments, such as telescopes, which must turn smoothly.

D.W./R.W.L.

The electric automobile (below) draws its electricity from a battery which it carries. Vehicles powered by electricity do not pollute the air with fumes, unlike some vehicles which burn certain types of gasoline or diesel oil.

ELECTROCARDIOGRAM (i lek′ trō kärd′ ē ə gram′) The electrocardiogram, abbreviated ECG or EKG, is a recording of the electrical activity of the heart muscle. The ECG from the normal heart shows impulses of a certain size and shape. When the heart muscle is not working properly because of disease or some other disorder, the ECG is changed. Such changes aid the doctor in making a diagnosis of why the heart is not beating normally.

The ECG is made by a machine called the electrocardiograph. This instrument has wires with electrodes at the ends. The electrodes are attached to the skin of the person. They pick up tiny changes in electrical activity from four points around the heart. These electrical impulses are sent through a voltage amplifier to make a recording by moving a pen across a strip of moving paper. Certain machines record the electrical activity on magnetic tape that can be played back for viewing on an oscilloscope.

P.G.C./J.J.F.

ELECTROCHEMISTRY (i lek′ trō kem′ ə strē) Electrochemistry is the branch of chemistry that deals with the chemical effects of electricity on substances. It also deals with the production of electricity in chemical reactions. These subjects are most easily studied in solutions of electrolytes. Electrolytes are substances that, when dissolved or melted, conduct electricity.

Electrochemistry involves the study of ions in gases, solutions, molten substances, and some crystals. The ions (atoms carrying an electrical charge) make it possible for electric currents to pass through these substances.

Another subject of electrochemistry is the conversion of chemical energy to electricity. This occurs in dry cells used in flashlights and in automobile batteries. (*See* BATTERY; CELL, ELECTRICAL.)

In electrolysis, electrical energy is used to produce chemical changes. Hydrogen, chlorine, and caustic soda are produced commercially by the electrolysis of salt water. Electrolysis is used in electroplating and in obtaining many metals from their ores.

Electrochemistry is also concerned with the study of corrosion. By studying corrosion processes, scientists can find ways to protect metals. In biochemistry, electrophoresis is used to analyze and separate proteins.

The study of electrochemistry is very important in science and industry because it explains the electrical effects and reactions that occur. J.J.A./A.D.

ELECTRODE (i lek′ trōd′) An electrode is the terminal of any electric source. In other words, an electrode is an electrical conductor by which an electric current enters or leaves a medium. (*See* CONDUCTION OF ELECTRICITY.) For example, in electrolysis, a current enters and leaves a solution by way of two electrodes, the anode and cathode. The anode is connected to the positive terminal of the electricity supply. The cathode is connected to the negative terminal of the supply. In an

In this electric furnace (below) the arc between two graphite electrodes provides the heat to melt iron, bronze, steel, and other metals and alloys. Another important use of electrodes is in electrolysis.

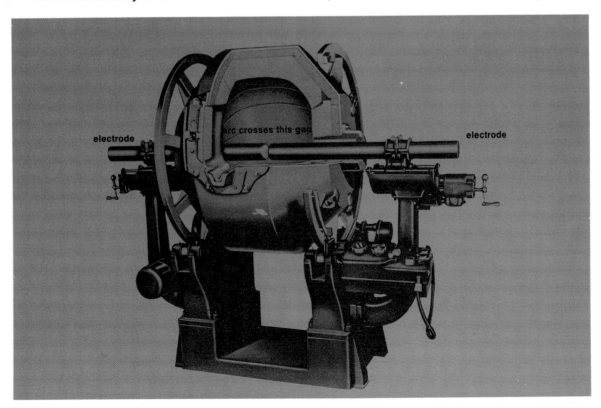

electric cell, the positive terminal is called the anode. The negative terminal is called the cathode. (*See* CELL, ELECTRICAL.) Electrons can flow from the cathode, through a circuit, to the anode. Some vacuum tubes, besides having a cathode and anode, have other electrodes called grids. Ordinary transistors have three electrodes called the emitter, base, and collector. *See also* ARC, ELECTRIC; CURRENT, ELECTRIC; FARADAY, MICHAEL.　　J.J.A./J.T.

ELECTROENCEPHALOGRAPH (i lek′ trō in sef′ ə lə graf′) The electroencephalograph is an instrument that measures and records electrical impulses from nerve cells in the brain. These recordings of the electrical activity of the brain, called electroencephalograms (abbreviated EEG) show the state of this activity. Normal EEG's have a frequency of 10 to 12 Hz. These are called alpha waves. Normal alpha waves occur when a person is awake and relaxed. When the person concentrates, the alpha waves decrease, giving way to smaller, faster waves.

During sleep, or when a person is unconscious, brain waves become very slow. Brain waves originate from the nerve cells in the brain. If these nerve cells become damaged by a head injury, by an infection in the brain, or by lack of oxygen, the EEG will be changed. Doctors have studied the EEG, and have learned how to diagnose epilepsy and to locate brain tumors.　　P.G.C./J.J.F.

ELECTROLYSIS (i lek′ träl′ ə səs) Electrolysis is the use of electricity to split up a substance into its different parts. Electrolysis can be used to extract metals from their ores. It can be used to purify metals. It can be used to prepare gases from liquids. Electrolysis is also used to put a layer of one metal closely on top of another. This is called electroplating.

Electrolysis only works with substances that can be dissolved or melted, and that will conduct an electric current. Substances that have these properties are called electrolytes.

When an electrolyte is melted or dissolved in water, its atoms or groups of atoms form ions. Ions are particles that bear electric charges. If the charges are positive, the ions are called cations. If they are negative charges, the ions are called anions. It is because they are electrically charged that ions can carry an electrical current through a solution. (*See* SOLUTION AND SOLUBILITY.) Hydrochloric acid is an electrolyte. It forms hydrogen ions with a positive charge, and chloride ions with a negative charge.

To electrolyze a substance, two electrodes are used. One is connected to the positive side of a battery or a DC electrical generator. The other is connected to the negative side. When the electrodes are dipped into the solution, the ions immediately start moving. The cations in the solution are attracted to the negative electrode (the cathode). The anions, with a negative charge, are attracted to the positive electrode (the anode).

When hydrochloric acid is electrolyzed, the hydrogen ions travel to the cathode, and the chloride ions travel to the anode. When the ions reach the electrodes, their electric charges are neutralized. The hydrogen ions become molecules of hydrogen gas, and the chloride ions become molecules of chlorine gas. Bubbles of the two different gases rise up from the electrodes.

When sodium chloride (common salt) is melted, it too can be electrolyzed. The result in this case is metallic sodium and chlorine gas. The sodium appears at the cathode, and chlorine bubbles up from the anode.

When a solution of sodium chloride is electrolyzed, the result is different. At the cathode, the sodium is released, but immediately it reacts with the water in the solution. This makes hydrogen gas and sodium hydroxide solution. At the anode, chlorine gas bubbles up as before.

Pure gases such as hydrogen, chlorine, and oxygen can easily be prepared by electrolysis. Pure metals such as sodium, potas-

ELECTROLYSIS OF MOLTEN SODIUM CHLORIDE

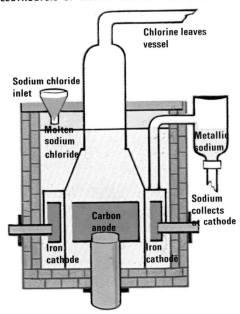

The diagrammatic cross section above shows the Downs cell. Molten, dry sodium chloride (salt) is split up into the elements sodium and chloride by passing an electric current through it. Sodium collects at the cathode and chlorine gas bubbles off at the anode. This reaction takes place on a commercial scale in the Downs cell.

ELECTROLYSIS OF IMPURE COPPER

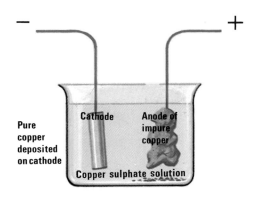

Electrolysis is used to refine copper. The cathode consists of a block of pure copper. A piece of impure copper forms the anode. The electrolyte is copper sulphate solution. The action of the current splits the electrolyte into copper and sulphate ions. The copper ions go to the cathode. Meanwhile, copper atoms in the anode become copper ions and move into the electrolyte to make up for the copper ions moving to the cathode. The impurities in the anode remain behind. Overall, pure copper is dissolved from the anode and built up on the cathode.

sium, and aluminum are also prepared in this way. Electrolysis is also a useful means of purifying, or refining, metals. Copper can be purified by using impure copper as the anode, and pure copper as the cathode. The electrolyte used is copper sulfate.

Electrolysis is often carried out in a special container. The container is called an electrolytic cell. The cell must be made of material that is strong enough to resist the attack of hot liquids. The temperatures reached in electrolysis are often very high. The electrolyte, and the substances that are made from it, may be very corrosive substances. The electrodes must also be made of special material. If they were not, they would be eaten away when they were dipped into the electrolyte. Sometimes expensive metals like platinum are used to make electrodes. Carbon rods may also be used.

The electrodes do not need to be two rods. One electrode is sometimes the lining of the electrolytic cell. In the special cell to make sodium hydroxide from sodium chloride solution, one electrode is a layer of mercury forming the floor of the cell. The sodium dissolves in the mercury. It forms an amalgam. From the amalgam, sodium hydroxide can be extracted later.

In 1832, the British scientist Michael Faraday stated two laws about electrolysis. The first law says that the amount of a substance that forms at an electrode is proportional to the quantity of electricity that is passed through the electrolytic cell. The second law says that when the same amount of electricity is passed through different electrolytes, the amounts of different substances that are formed are proportional to their equivalent weights.   D.W./A.D.

ELECTROMAGNETIC RADIATION (i lek′ trō mag net′ ik rād′ ē ā′ shən) There are many different kinds of electromagnetic radiation. Two very important kinds are light and radio waves. We need light to see things by. We use radio waves to send messages and for broadcasting. There are also other types of electromagnetic radiation. In fact, there is a complete range. The range is called the electromagnetic spectrum. The radiation with the most energy is called gamma rays. Then come X rays and ultraviolet rays. Next comes light, then infrared rays. The radiation with the least energy consists of microwaves and radio waves.

All electromagnetic radiation is made up of waves. They are produced by electrically charged particles. An electron is such a particle. These particles have an electric field. They move very fast. Because of this, they also have a magnetic field. (*See* ELECTROMAGNETISM.) Sometimes their speeds change. They are accelerated. Then their fields change as well. The particles move to and fro. They are said to vibrate. These vibrations form a wave. The wave moves away from the particles.

The fields vibrate at right angles to the direction of the wave. Therefore the waves are called transverse waves. The fields also vibrate at right angles to each other.

Some waves, like sound, need some material, like the air, to move in. The material is called the medium. Electromagnetic radiation does not need any medium. It can travel in a vacuum. It moves faster in a vacuum than in any medium. In a vacuum, its speed is 299,790 km [186,281 mi] per second. This is called "the speed of light."

Discovery of electromagnetic waves The existence of electromagnetic waves was first suggested by a Scottish mathematician in 1864. His name was James Clerk Maxwell. He also predicted radio waves. These waves were discovered in 1887 by a German physicist, Heinrich Hertz. Ten years later X rays and gamma rays were discovered. They were

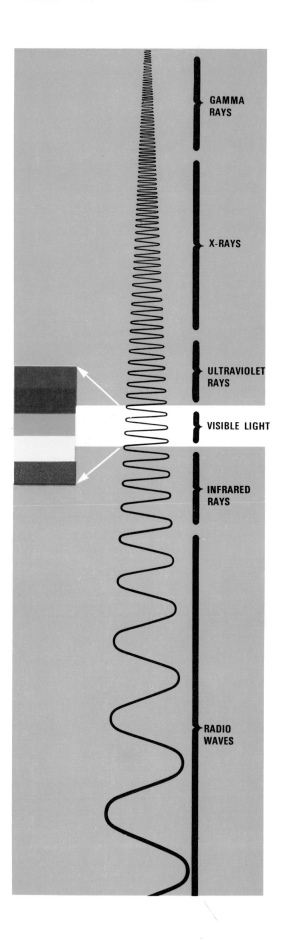

The visible light spectrum (right) is only a part of the entire electromagnetic radiation spectrum.

GAMMA RAYS

X-RAYS

ULTRAVIOLET RAYS

VISIBLE LIGHT

INFRARED RAYS

RADIO WAVES

being given off by radioactive atoms. (*See* RADIOACTIVITY.) Soon they were shown to be electromagnetic radiation. Early in this century the quantum theory was worked out. It explains electromagnetic radiation very well. Now we know that all electromagnetic radiation is given off in "packets." These packets are packets of energy. They are called quanta. Electromagnetic radiation is also absorbed in quanta. M.E./J.T.

ELECTROMAGNETISM

The word electromagnetism(i lek′ trō mag′ nə tiz′ əm) means two things. It is the magnetism produced by an electric current. It is also a branch of physics that studies the connections between electricity and magnetism. The study of electromagnetism began in the early 19th century. A Danish scientist named Hans Christian Oersted placed a magnetic needle near a wire that had a current flowing through it. He noticed that when the current flowed, the needle was deflected. He realized that the current was producing a magnetic field.

An electric current is caused by the movement of electrons through a wire. These electrons are very tiny particles and they have an electric charge. Any charged object produces an electric field. (*See* ELECTROSTATICS.) This field extends outward from the charge. It can be represented by lines of force. Suppose a second charged body is put near the first one. This body will be attracted or repelled. The lines of force show the direction in which it tends to move. For a wire with a current passing through it, these lines go outward at right angles. A charged body has an electric field around it whether the charges are moving or not. But if the charges are moving, then the body also has a magnetic field. Magnetism is always caused by moving electric charges. A current is caused by elec-

trons flowing through the wire. Because these electrons are moving, they set up a magnetic field around the wire. The magnetic field can also be represented by lines of force. These lines form rings around the wire.

This can be shown very easily. Suppose you have a single strand of wire passing through a card. The wire and the card are at right angles. Some iron filings are scattered on the card. Iron filings are very small pieces of iron. A current is then passed through the wire. Iron is magnetic and tends to line up with a magnetic field. So the iron filings form rings around the wire. They have arranged themselves along the lines of force of the magnetic field. This shows the shape of the magnetic field around the wire. The strength of the field increases as the current in the wire gets stronger. It also varies with the distance from the wire. The further away the field, the weaker it gets.

A strong magnetic field can be made by passing a current through a solenoid. A solenoid is a long coil of insulated wire wound around a tube. When a current is passed through it, each turn of the coil produces a magnetic field. A solenoid usually has many turns, each producing a magnetic field. These fields combine to form a large magnetic field. The solenoid behaves rather like a bar magnet. It has a north pole and a south pole. The field can be increased by putting an iron bar

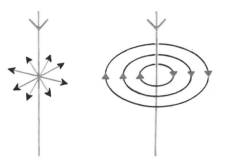

When an electric current is passed through a straight conductor, radial lines (left) of electrical force and circular lines (right) of magnetic force are set up at the same time around the straight conductor.

Rolls of steel sheet (above) are being lifted by a powerful electromagnet. Electromagnets are able to handle bulky objects made of iron and steel.

inside the solenoid. The iron becomes magnetized. Its field combines with the field caused by the current to form an even larger field. A solenoid with an iron bar inside it is known as an electromagnet. The first electromagnet was built in England in 1825 by William Sturgeon.

Electromagnets are very powerful. Since they have a magnetic field, they can be used to lift heavy iron and steel objects. An early electromagnet was built by Joseph Henry for the College of New Jersey (now Princeton University). It could lift 350 kg [770 lbs].

Large electromagnets produce a great amount of heat and they have to be kept cool. To do this, pipes carrying cold water are placed in the coil. In some electromagnets, the coil is made of hollow wires through which water can flow. The National Magnet Laboratory at the Massachusetts Institute of Technology has a very large electromagnet. It uses 16 million watts of electric power and needs 7,571 l [2,000 gal] of water every minute to keep it cool.

Electromagnetism is also concerned with using a magnetic field to make an electric current. This can be done by moving a piece of wire in a magnetic field. Moving the wire causes a current to flow in it. The current is said to be induced. (*See* INDUCTION.)

Uses of electromagnetism A country's electricity supply is produced by generators. These generators use mechanical power to produce electricity. A coil of wire is spun between the poles of a magnet. This induces a current in the wire. Sometimes the magnet is spun around the coil. An electromagnet can be used to magnetize steel. The iron inside a solenoid becomes magnetized when the solenoid is switched on. When it is switched off, the iron loses its magnetism. If a steel bar is put inside a solenoid, it too becomes magnetized. But when the current in the solenoid is switched off, the steel keeps some of its magnetism. Permanent magnets can be made in this way.

Powerful electromagnets are used in industry to lift iron and steel. They are also used for separating iron and steel from nonmagnetic metals like copper and brass. These metals are not attracted to a magnet.

The loudspeaker in a radio contains an electromagnet. It converts the electric signal into a mechanical force. This force is then used to produce sounds. In tape recorders, the tape is magnetized by a small electromagnet.

Particle accelerators are very large machines used in nuclear physics research. These accelerators use large electromagnets to make subatomic particles travel very fast. (*See* ACCELERATOR, PARTICLE.) There is an accelerator at Berkeley, California. Its electromagnet weighs over 4,000 tons. Its coil contains about 300 tons of copper.

Scientists are trying to use nuclear fusion to produce energy. The temperatures reached during fusion are very high indeed. They are so high that no substance can possibly withstand them. This means that the reacting gases cannot yet be confined. Scientists are looking at ways of using an electromagnetic field to do this. If the gases could be confined, then the fusion reaction could be controlled. Fusion reactors would supply almost limitless energy and solve the problem of the shortage of fuel.

M.E./A.I.

ELECTROMOTIVE FORCE (i lek′ trə mōt′ iv fōrs′) An electric circuit always contains a device that makes the charges move. This device provides the power for the circuit and is said to have an electromotive force. Electromotive force is usually shortened to EMF. Its strength is measured in volts. (*See* VOLTAGE.) The most common devices for providing an EMF are the electric cell and the generator. In an electric cell, an EMF is produced by chemical action. In a generator, electromagnetism is used to produce an EMF. Sometimes other methods are used. For example, heat can be used to produce an EMF. This can be done by putting a thermocouple into a circuit. If one of its junctions is heated, a current flows. Many kinds of photoelectric devices give an EMF when light shines on them. (*See* PHOTOELECTRIC EFFECT.) Another device that can be used is the fuel cell. Like the electric cell, it uses chemical action to produce an EMF. It may someday be used to power electric cars. M.E./J.T.

ELECTROMOTIVE SERIES (i lek′ trə mōt′ iv sir′ ēz) The electromotive series is a list of metals that shows how reactive they are. At the top of the list are the most reactive metals. Potassium is the first, followed by sodium. These are so reactive that they will even burst into flame when put into water. They are nearly always found as salts.

At the bottom of the list are the metals that react least with other substances. Platinum and gold will not even react with strong acids. Metals low on the list do not corrode readily. (*See* CORROSION.)

A metal high on the list will throw out, or

displace, a metal lower on the list from its salts. For example, iron is higher in the series than copper. So, if a piece of iron is dipped into a solution of copper sulfate, the copper is displaced. It forms a coating on the iron. At the same time, the iron turns into iron sulfate and dissolves.

The electromotive series is useful for predicting when two metals put close together will undergo corrosion. For example, if a nut is made from an element high in the series, and it is used with a bolt made from a metal much lower in the series, this is bad. After a while, corrosion will occur. The nut will gradually be eaten away. Engineers are always careful when they must use two metals together.

The electromotive series is also useful for telling how two different metals will act if they are used as the plates of a battery. The metal higher in the series always becomes the negative pole of the battery, while the lower metal becomes positive. The voltage that a battery produces depends upon the distance between the metals in the series. The greater the distance, the higher the voltage. *See also* REACTION, PRINCIPLE OF. D.W./A.D.

ELECTRON (i lek′ trän′) An electron is a subatomic particle that has a negative electric charge. An electron has an extremely small mass. It has about 1/1836 the mass of a hydrogen atom.

The atoms of all elements contain electrons. The negative charge of the electron is balanced by an equal number of positively-charged protons in the atom. The protons are in the nucleus of the atom, and the electrons orbit around them. Each chemical element requires a specific number of electrons and protons in order to remain neutral. This number is called the atomic number of the element.

We have used our knowledge of electrons to make many devices. Electric current is actually the flow of electrons through a wire.

An electron microscope works using a beam of electrons. The electron was discovered by the British physicist Sir J. J. Thomson, in 1897. J.M.C./A.D.

ELECTRONIC MUSIC (i lek′ trän′ ik myü′zik) Electronic music is made up of sounds that are produced by special electronic equipment, not by the musical instruments we usually hear in live performances or on records and tapes.

The basic unit of the special equipment is usually an oscillator. It produces sounds within the range of human hearing when its signal is sent through an amplifier and played back to the listener through a loudspeaker or headphones. More complicated instruments can be constructed by using many oscillators that produce a variety of sounds. These sounds can imitate those of traditional musical instruments, or they can be new and different from the usual musical sounds.

Musicians have different opinions about the uses of electronic music. A composer can write down the ''notes'' that he wants the electronic devices to produce. He has a wide choice of sounds that can be varied in pitch, loudness, duration, and other musical characteristics. He can even make electronic ''noise'' if his composition requires it. He can put the sounds of his composition together using a computer, or with a special device called a synthesizer. Whenever the composition is played for the listener, it will be exactly the same. It cannot be changed from one performance to the next by different musicians.

On the other hand, the musician can use his electronic instruments to experiment with musical sounds. He can mix the sounds in many different ways using a synthesizer. He can play someone else's composition, but change the sounds of the notes to suit himself. He can improvise and make new sounds as he plays along. He can conduct experiments with listeners to find out which sounds the listeners prefer and in which arrangements. He can add

This electronic synthesizer can create sounds that resemble those of musical instruments or the human voice.

or subtract parts of the sound to determine when the listener can just notice that the sound has changed.

In the sound laboratory or in the concert hall, the field of electronics has made possible the study of musical sounds from many different points of view.   P.G.C./L.L.R.

ELECTRONICS (i lek′ trän′ iks) Electronics is a vital part of our daily lives. Cheap electronic equipment means that almost every home in richer countries has a television set. Radios are common in most parts of the world. Without electronic hearing aids, many deaf people would hear nothing. People with heart diseases use electronic devices called pacemakers to keep their hearts beating. Without them, the people would die. Electronic equipment such as X ray machines are widely used in hospitals.

History of electronics   The science of electronics is about a hundred years old. An important piece of equipment in the history of electronics is the cathode-ray tube. This is a glass tube that has two electrodes in it. These electrodes can be joined into an electric circuit. When it is switched on, the current flows from one electrode to the other. There is only a very small amount of air inside the tube. If there were too much air inside, the molecules of the air would stop the flow of current.

The first discovery in electronics was made by Sir William Crookes in 1879. He showed that when a current flows in the cathode-ray tube, the negative electrode gives off rays. He called them cathode rays, since the negative electrode is called the cathode. In 1897, Sir J. J. Thomson discovered the electron. He also discovered that cathode rays were streams of electrons.

The next important step came in 1883. The American scientist, Thomas Edison, put a metal plate inside a light bulb. The plate was positively charged. When the light bulb was switched on, the filament glowed as usual. But Edison found that electricity was flowing from the filament to the metal plate. This is called thermionic emission. John Fleming put this effect to practical use. In 1904, he used the effect to build the first vacuum tube. It is called the diode because it has two electrodes. Three years later, Lee de Forest invented a different kind of vacuum tube, called a triode. A triode has a metal grid between the two electrodes. The grid is used to vary the strength of the electric current between the two electrodes. By this means, it amplifies, or makes stronger, the electric current and power. (*See* AMPLIFIER.) The diode and triode were used in the development of radio sets and telephones.

Two other vacuum tube devices are the magnetron and the klystron. They were invented in 1939 and were quickly used in the invention of radar. Radar is used to detect objects and find out how far away they are. It sends out radio waves. If the waves hit an object, they are reflected back. The radar set picks up these reflected waves and so detects the object. Radar can only detect objects above a certain size. If the radio waves have shorter wavelengths, then smaller objects can be detected. Magnetrons and klystrons pro-

Circuits being tested at the rate of 30 a minute in an electronics factory are shown above.

duce radio waves with very short wavelengths.

Meanwhile, the cathode ray tube was being improved. In 1926, John Logie Baird used it in his invention of the television. Later they were used in other electronic devices.

Modern electronics A major breakthrough in electronics occurred in 1947 when William Shockley invented the transistor. This tiny device can do everything a vacuum tube could do. It is both a rectifier (changing alternating current to direct current) and an amplifier. Transistors have many advantages. They weigh less than an ounce and take up very little space. They are sturdy and durable. And they use very little power to do their work.

The first transistors were made of crystals of germanium, a metallic element. Then it was found that silicon could serve as well as germanium. This was fortunate because silicon is so plentiful. It exists in nature as silicon dioxide, ordinary sand. Using silicon, laboratories could make thousands of transistors quickly and inexpensively. This was important because in the 1950s and 1960s the U. S. Government's space program needed thousands of transistors. So did the computer industry. Transistors also were used in radios, record players, television sets, hearing aids, and many other devices.

The availability of the transistor put in motion a dramatic shift toward miniaturization of electronic devices. This started in the mid-1960s when several laboratories developed the integrated electronic circuit. This device consists of a single miniaturized silicon component that combines the functions of several individual components. Among these individual components are interconnected transistors. This accomplishment was only the beginning. Before the end of the decade, large-scale integration (LSI) had emerged. Techniques were soon found whereby hundreds and even thousands of electronic circuits could be put on a single silicon wafer, or chip, about the size of a quarter.

To produce these miniature marvels, engineers first make a drawing of the electronic circuitry on mylar sheets several hundred times the size of the final product. These sheets are later reduced in size photographically. They are then printed on chemically treated silicon chips and further processed. The finished product is a true miniature of the original drawing. Some of these chips can pass throught the eye of a needle with room to spare.

Application of the integrated circuit to computer design pointed the way toward miniaturization of computers. The room-sized monsters of the early days gave way to less cumbersome transistorized models. The use of integrated circuits gave rise to still smaller desk-top models called minicomputers. But when Marcian E. (Ted) Hoff, Jr. came up with a new concept for the design of LSI chips in 1969, unbelievably small computers became a possibility. He condensed all of the computer's arithmetic so it could fit on just one chip. This silicon chip, called a microprocessor, was a boon to the computer industry. It is the heart of the small computer. Because of this invention, home computers, video games, and pocket calculators became

These devices are called programmable controllers. They are industrial computers that can be programmed to perform a series of commands to operate various machines and processes.

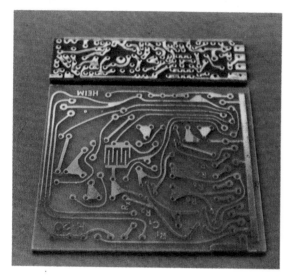

An enlarged gold-plated printed circuit, for use in equipment such as televisions, is pictured above.

a reality. The applications of Hoff's invention are endless.

Hooking his microprocessor to a data chip and a control chip gave Hoff his microcomputer. It was about the size of a jelly bean. It could perform 10,000 calculations per second. That performance equals what the monstrous ENIAC could do with its 18,000 vacuum tubes. A big advantage of the microcomputer is its flexibility. Changing its memory chip changes its program.

This space-saving computer is invaluable to space technology. The success of the totally computerized space shuttle *Columbia* makes this point. National defense and military and civil aviation also use this device. Thousands of automated industrial and business operations will be able to cut costs through its use. M.E./L.L.R.

ELECTRON MICROSCOPE (i lek' trän' mī' krə skōp') An electron microscope is a microscope that can magnify objects over a half million times. (*See* MAGNIFICATION.) An electron microscope works on a principle similar to that of a regular light microscope. In a light microscope, a bright light is directed through a specimen (object to be magnified) and into the microscope's objective lens. The light rays are focused by the lens, producing a magnified image. (*See* LENS.)

In an electron microscope, a beam of fast-moving electrons is passed through a very thin slice of the specimen. The electrons are focused by magnetic lenses onto a fluorescent screen. (*See* FLUORESCENCE.) On the screen, the magnified image can be observed directly or photographed.

Scanning electron microscope A scanning electron microscope works in the same way as a television camera. (*See* TELEVISION.) A scanning electron microscope scans the surface of a specimen with a fine beam of electrons. A picture is obtained that shows detail of the specimen's surface.

Through the use of electron microscopes,

A scanning electron microscope moves a beam of electrons across a specimen. The electrons then pass through a collector and the magnified image is formed on a television screen such as the one shown above.

scientists have obtained much new knowledge about viruses, bacteria, and other microscopic forms of life. The scientists who work with electron microscopes are called electron microscopists. Electron microscopes are found in many hospitals, universities, and laboratories. *See also* ELECTRON.

J.M.C./S.S.B.

Photographs taken by means of electron microscopes are known as electron micrographs. Shown above are two examples of micrographs, taken with the type of electron microscope that scans the object in the way that a television camera scans a scene. The micrographs show the contrast in structure between natural and synthetic fibers. Left, a fiber of wool; right, a nonwoven fabric made of Heterofil fibers, showing the detail of the bond between the fibers.

ELECTRON VOLT (i lek′ trän′ vōlt′) An electron volt is a measurement of nuclear energy. It is the energy gained by an electron when it passes from one point to another point that is one volt higher in potential. One electron volt is equal to approximately 1.6×10^{-19} joules. The burning of one atom of carbon in coal or oil produces about three electron volts of energy. The fissioning of one uranium nucleus produces about 200 million electron volts. (*See* FISSION.)   W.R.P./J.T.

ELECTROPHORESIS (i lek′ trə fə rē′ səs) Electrophoresis is a method sometimes used to separate the particles of different substances in a solution. (*See* SOLUTION AND SOLUBILITY.) An electric current is passed through the solution from one electrode to another. Many substances are made of particles that have an electric charge. When the electric current passes, the particles are attracted to one of the electrodes. They gradually move through the solution.

The speed at which the particles move depends upon how big they are, and what size of electric charge they have. By switching off the current after a certain time, it is possible to separate different particles in a solution. Modern methods of electrophoresis use wet filter paper or plates of gelatine instead of a container of water.

Electrophoresis has been used to separate the different proteins in the blood. It has been used to detect disease. It can be used to detect the presence of drugs and poisons in the body.

D.M.H.W./A.D.

ELECTROPLATING (i lek′ trə plāt′ ing) Electroplating is a method of coating an article with a thin layer of metal. Usually the article itself is also made of metal. When an article is coated with a metal, it is said to be plated. In electroplating, the coating is done by electrolysis.

In electrolysis, two electrodes are placed in a liquid. A current is then passed through the liquid from one electrode to the other. In electroplating, the article and the metal that forms the coating are used as electrodes. They are placed in a solution of a compound of the metal. (*See* SOLUTION AND SOLUBILITY.) Usually this compound is a salt. The article and the metal are then connected to a supply of DC electricity. The positive side of the supply is attached to the metal and the negative side to the article. The current flows from the metal, through the solution, to the article. As the current flows, the metal electrode is gradually "eaten away." The metal goes into the solution and comes out of the solution onto the article.

For example, suppose you want to coat a brass faucet with nickel. The faucet and the

The metal parts (left) will be plated with zinc in this programmed, automated electroplating system.

nickel would be used as electrodes. Usually a salt of nickel called nickel sulfate is used as the solution. When the current is switched on, the faucet gradually becomes coated with brilliant nickel plate.

Electroplating was first done about a hundred years ago. The first metal to be used for coating was silver. A cheap metal could be coated and made to look as if it were made out of silver. Spoons, forks, and other articles were coated in this way. Silver-plated articles look as if they were made of solid silver. But, of course, they are much cheaper to produce. Such articles are stamped with the letters E.P.N.S. This stands for Electroplated Nickel Silver. If they were not stamped, people might think that they were solid silver.

Articles are often plated with chromium. Chromium is much harder than other metals and also prevents rusting. Therefore, chromium-plated articles last longer. Automobile bumpers are made out of steel. They are then plated with copper, followed by nickel, and then by chromium.

The thickness of the coating varies. It depends on the article to be coated and on the metal used. In silver plating, the coating is only 1/2000 mm [0.00002 in]. A recent development in electroplating is called "hard chromium" plating. Here, a much thicker layer of chromium is used than would be normal. It is about 1/50 mm [0.0008 in] thick. This process is used to restore machine parts. It is also used to plate the tips of tools, such as drills. It makes them last longer.

Materials other than metals can also be electroplated. Most other materials do not conduct electricity. They have to be coated with a thin layer of graphite first. Graphite is a form of carbon and conducts electricity. This method is sometimes used to coat plaster casts with copper. M.E./A.D.

Above, the gold-leaf electroscope.

ELECTROSCOPE (i lek′ trə skōp′) The electroscope is an instrument used to detect electric charge. (*See* CHARGE, ELECTRIC.) The electroscope can also be used to tell whether the charge is positive or negative. Electroscopes can also detect X rays and other electromagnetic radiation.

The gold-leaf electroscope is a common type of electroscope. In 1787, Abraham Bennet, a British scientist, invented the gold-leaf electroscope. The instrument consists of two slender strips of gold foil hanging from a metal rod. The metal rod acts as a conductor. (*See* CONDUCTION OF ELECTRICITY.) A nonconductor, such as wood, holds the conductor in a stand. The stand is often made of glass.

When the conductor has no electric charge, the foil strips hang straight down. If the conductor is charged with electricity, the strips become charged. Both strips receive the same kind of charge. Because bodies with like charges repel each other, the strips move apart. The amount of movement gives an indication of the strength of the charge. The electroscope can be used to measure high voltages. William Henly, a British scientist, converted an electroscope into an electrometer by adding a scale of numbers to it. An elec-trometer measures the strength of electric charges.

To find out whether a charge is positive or negative, the activated electroscope is tested with a known charge. For example, if a known positive charge makes the foil strips fall back together, the unknown charge is negative. Opposite charges neutralize each other. If the strips spread further apart, the unknown charge is positive. *See also* ELECTROSTATICS.   J.J.A./J.T.

ELECTROSTATICS (i lek′ trə stat′ iks) Electric charges can be either moving or still. For example, in an electric circuit the charges are moving in the wire. If an object is rubbed, it sometimes gains an electric charge. In this case the charges are not moving. They are said to be static. The electricity is called static electricity. The study of static electricity is called electrostatics.

When materials like amber are rubbed, they are able to attract light objects such as feathers. The ancient Greeks knew this. In the 1500s, William Gilbert found that many other materials behaved in the same way when rubbed. He called this effect electric, after the Greek word *elektron*, which means amber. He found, for example, that glass could be electrified by rubbing it with silk. However, he could not find a way to electrify metals. In 1729, Stephen Gray discovered another difference between metals and other materials. He found that electricity can flow along metals but not along nonmetals. Metals are said to conduct electricity and are called conductors. Conductors other than metals have been discovered since then. One such conductor is graphite. Materials in which electricity does not flow are called insulators.

A very important discovery was made in France around 1733 by the scientist Charles DuFay. He found that there are two different kinds of electric charge. They are called positive charge and negative charge. He found that bodies having the same kind of charge

Lightning results from a great natural build-up of static electricity. 1. An electrical charge (usually negative) accumulates on the underside of a thundercloud. Attracted by this negative charge, a positive electrical charge accumulates on high objects beneath the cloud. 2 and 3. As the build-up of electrostatic charges goes on, "leader streams"

of electric current are sent down from the cloud, and up from high points on the ground. 4. Finally, the electrical resistance of the air between the ground and the cloud is broken down. At this point, a flash of lightning is seen bridging the gap between cloud and ground. The cloud has momentarily lost its electric charge as this happens.

repelled, or pushed each other away. Bodies with opposite charges attracted each other. In both cases, there is a force acting between the two bodies. The English scientist Joseph Priestley studied this force. He found that for spherical objects the strength of the force depends on the distance between the two bodies. He made this discovery in 1766. He showed that the electric force obeys the inverse square law. This law says that the force increases as the two bodies get closer together. If the distance between the two is halved, the force becomes four times as strong. (*See* INVERSE SQUARE LAW.)

In 1787, a very important instrument was invented. It is called the the gold-leaf electroscope and is used to detect electric charge. It was soon used to investigate the charge on a hollow body. The electroscope showed that all the charge lies on the outside surface. The inside surface has no charge at all.

Scientists still did not know what electricity was. They thought that it was like a liquid. We know now that many electric effects are caused by very small particles called electrons. Electrons are negatively charged and are found in atoms. An atom has a heavy core called a nucleus. Surrounding this core there are a number of electrons. When two materials are rubbed together, the electrons are sometimes pulled out of the atoms. They get transferred from one material to another. When glass is rubbed with silk, the electrons move from the glass to the silk. Since the electrons have a negative charge, the silk becomes negatively charged. The glass has lost electrons, so it gains a positive charge. Ebonite can become charged by being rubbed with fur. In this case, the electrons move from the fur to the ebonite. The ebonite becomes negatively charged and the fur positively charged.

The SI unit of electric charge is called the coulomb. It is the amount of electricity that a current of one ampere transfers in one second. (*See* INTERNATIONAL SYSTEM.)

The electric field If a body has a charge, it is said to be surrounded by an electric, or electrostatic, field. When another charged body is placed near the first body, it is affected by the field. The field produces a force on the body. The body is either attracted or repelled. A large charge sets up a strong electric field. The strength of the field varies from point to point. It is strongest nearest the body causing it. Further away, the field gets weaker.

A useful idea is to imagine the field as lines of force. These lines show the direction in which a positive charge would move in the field. For a round body, the lines of force of its field are straight lines. If its charge is positive, they go outward from the charge evenly in every direction. They go outward because a positive charge repels, or pushes away, another positive charge. If the charge is negative, the lines go in the opposite direction. They go inward to the charge. This shows that it attracts a positive charge. As the lines of force move away from the body, they spread out. The field also becomes weaker. Similarly, near the body the lines are close together and the field is strong. In other words the strength of the field is related to the density of the lines.

For a sphere that is a conductor, the charge is spread evenly over the surface. Suppose the charged body is not a sphere, but is shaped like a football. This shape is curved most at the ends. Most of the charges are gathered at the ends. This means that the electric field depends on the shape of the body causing it. The field is strongest where the body curves most. For a sphere, the electrostatic field has the same strength all around it. Its strength changes only as you move away from the sphere. For a body shaped like a football, the field is greatest at either end.

Electrostatic charging We have already come across one way of charging an object. This is by rubbing it with something. Not all objects can be charged like this, though.

Another way is by touching it with a charged body. A third method is called induction. With induction, no contact is made with another body.

Imagine two metal balls touching each other but insulated from everything else. They could be placed on the end of glass rods, for example. The rods could then be held in the hand and the balls would be insulated. An ebonite rod with a negative charge is then brought close to one of them. The ebonite repels the electrons in that ball and they move to the ball that is further away. This ball becomes negatively charged because the electrons have a negative charge. The ball near the rod has a positive charge because it has lost some electrons. They remain charged as long as the rod is held in place. When the rod is taken away, they lose their charges because the electrons flow back again. Suppose the rod is kept in place and the balls are separated. They stay charged because the rod is still there. But now, if the rod is removed, the electrons cannot flow back. There is no contact between the balls. The two balls have been charged by induction. One has a positive charge and the other a negative charge.

Electric charge can be stored in capacitors. These are made out of two conductors placed close together but not touching. Usually a capacitor has two pieces of metal foil separated by some insulating material. One way to charge a capacitor is by connecting it to a battery. The battery sets up a potential difference across the capacitor. This causes the pieces of foil in the capacitor to have opposite charges. These charges remain there when the battery is removed. M.E./A.I.

ELEMENT

Elements (el′ ə mənts) are the simple materials from which everything in the universe is made. An element is made of atoms. In any element there are only atoms of one kind. An element cannot be broken down into anything else but its own kind of atoms in a chemical reaction. There are over 90 different elements that occur in nature. Some of them are very common. Carbon, for example, is an element that is found in every living animal and plant.

Elements can occur by themselves. A pure metal such as gold consists of only atoms of gold. It is an element. Pure hydrogen gas is another element that can exist by itself. In nature, however, elements are usually found linked to other elements. When two or more different elements are linked together they form a chemical compound. Water, for example, is a compound of the elements hydrogen and oxygen. Sodium chloride (common salt) is a compound of the two elements sodium and chlorine.

Elements can mix together without having to form a compound. Air is a mixture of the elements nitrogen, oxygen, and argon. It is not a compound, because the elements are not joined together chemically.

Kinds of elements   There are two ways of classifying elements. One way is to divide them into metals and non-metals. Metals make up more than three-quarters of all the elements. However, many of the non-metallic elements are abundant in nature. Oxygen, hydrogen, carbon, and silicon are very common non-metallic elements.

The other way of classifying elements is to divide them into solids, liquids, and gases at normal temperature and pressure. If this is done, most elements are found to be solids. Bromine and mercury are liquids. The elements oxygen and nitrogen are gases.

Chemical names and symbols   Every element has its own name and a chemical symbol. The name of the element often gives a clue to what sort of substance it is. Nearly all of the metallic elements have the ending -ium, for example. Some of the metals which have been known for a very long time do not end with -ium. Gold, zinc, iron, and nickel were in use long before the custom was adopted.

Most of the elements have names that come from Latin and Greek words. Hydrogen comes from the Greek for watermaker, because it can be burned to make water. Krypton comes from the Greek for concealed, because it was so hard to discover in the atmosphere. Bromine was named for the Greek for stench, because of its bad smell. Some elements are named for places or for scientists. Francium is named for France, and einsteinium, nobelium, and curium for the scientists Einstein, Nobel, and Curie.

The symbol of an element is a kind of shorthand for the name. The symbols are either one or two letters. Often the symbol comes from the English name. Thus O stands for oxygen and S for sulfur. It may come from the Latin name, like Na for sodium (natrium) and Ag for silver (argentum).

The abundance of the elements   The most abundant element in the universe is the gaseous element hydrogen. The sun and the stars consist mostly of this element. In the earth's crust, the most abundant element is oxygen. Oxygen is found in the atmosphere, in the oceans as water, and in many minerals. Next most abundant is silicon. Silicon is found in nearly every rock found on earth, except for limestone.

Some elements are very rare. Radium is one example. It is one of the radioactive elements. Radioactive elements are rare because they gradually change into different elements. Radium eventually changes into the more common element lead. This kind of change is called radioactive decay. To obtain just one-tenth of a gram of radium, Marie and Pierre Curie had to work hard for many months. They had to extract it from several tons of the rocky ore called pitchblende.

Atomic structure   All elements are made of atoms. It is the way that their atoms differ that makes every element different. To understand how one atom is different from another, it is necessary to understand what an atom is made of. Atoms are made of small particles. These are called subatomic particles. It is the number of particles that makes one atom different from another.

In the center of every atom is a group of particles. Some of them are protons. They have a positive electric charge. The rest are neutrons. They have no electric charge. Together these particles make up the nucleus of the atom. Outside the nucleus are electrons. These are particles with a negative electric charge. The number of electrons in an atom is the same as the number of protons. The positive and negative electric charges balance one another, so that each atom is electrically neutral.

The number of protons in the nucleus of an atom is called the atomic number. It is the same in all the atoms of one element. It identifies that element. Every atom with the atomic number 6 is a carbon atom, for example. The number of neutrons in the nucleus is not always the same. Atoms which have the same atomic number but different numbers of neutrons are called isotopes of the same element.

Orbital electrons   Each atom has orbital electrons around its nucleus. The electrons move in what are called electron shells. The shells are arranged at different distances from the nucleus. Nearest to the nucleus is the first shell. The first shell may contain up to two electrons, but no more. Further out is the second shell. This may contain up to eight electrons. The third shell may contain up to 18 electrons.

The simplest element is hydrogen. It has the atomic number 1. In its nucleus is just one proton. It has one electron circling the nucleus, in the first shell. The element with

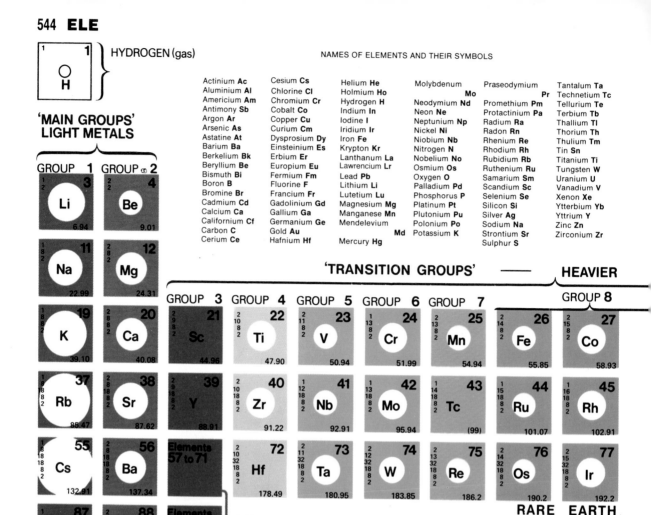

HYDROGEN (gas)

NAMES OF ELEMENTS AND THEIR SYMBOLS

Actinium **Ac**
Aluminium **Al**
Americium **Am**
Antimony **Sb**
Argon **Ar**
Arsenic **As**
Astatine **At**
Barium **Ba**
Berkelium **Bk**
Beryllium **Be**
Bismuth **Bi**
Boron **B**
Bromine **Br**
Cadmium **Cd**
Calcium **Ca**
Californium **Cf**
Carbon **C**
Cerium **Ce**

Cesium **Cs**
Chlorine **Cl**
Chromium **Cr**
Cobalt **Co**
Copper **Cu**
Curium **Cm**
Dysprosium **Dy**
Einsteinium **Es**
Erbium **Er**
Europium **Eu**
Fermium **Fm**
Fluorine **F**
Francium **Fr**
Gadolinium **Gd**
Gallium **Ga**
Germanium **Ge**
Gold **Au**
Hafnium **Hf**

Helium **He**
Holmium **Ho**
Hydrogen **H**
Indium **In**
Iodine **I**
Iridium **Ir**
Iron **Fe**
Krypton **Kr**
Lanthanum **La**
Lawrencium **Lr**
Lead **Pb**
Lithium **Li**
Lutetium **Lu**
Magnesium **Mg**
Manganese **Mn**
Mendelevium **Md**
Mercury **Hg**

Molybdenum **Mo**
Neodymium **Nd**
Neon **Ne**
Neptunium **Np**
Nickel **Ni**
Niobium **Nb**
Nitrogen **N**
Nobelium **No**
Osmium **Os**
Oxygen **O**
Palladium **Pd**
Phosphorus **P**
Platinum **Pt**
Plutonium **Pu**
Polonium **Po**
Potassium **K**

Praseodymium **Pr**
Promethium **Pm**
Protactinium **Pa**
Radium **Ra**
Radon **Rn**
Rhenium **Re**
Rhodium **Rh**
Rubidium **Rb**
Ruthenium **Ru**
Samarium **Sm**
Scandium **Sc**
Selenium **Se**
Silicon **Si**
Silver **Ag**
Sodium **Na**
Strontium **Sr**
Sulphur **S**

Tantalum **Ta**
Technetium **Tc**
Tellurium **Te**
Terbium **Tb**
Thallium **Tl**
Thorium **Th**
Thulium **Tm**
Tin **Sn**
Titanium **Ti**
Tungsten **W**
Uranium **U**
Vanadium **V**
Xenon **Xe**
Ytterbium **Yb**
Yttrium **Y**
Zinc **Zn**
Zirconium **Zr**

atomic number 2 is helium. It has two protons in its nucleus. Around this, two electrons orbit. They fill up the first shell. Element number 3 is lithium. It has three protons in its nucleus, so it must have three electrons in orbit. Two of them are in the first shell, and the other one is in the second shell. As the atomic number of the element increases, the shells fill up. Element number 11 is sodium. It has two electrons in the first shell

(full), eight in the second shell (full), and one in the third shell, making 11.

Properties of the elements   The properties of the elements depend upon the arrangement of the electrons in their shells. This is because when atoms of elements react with others, electrons form bonds between them. Elements with full outer shells tend to be inert. They do not easily make compounds with

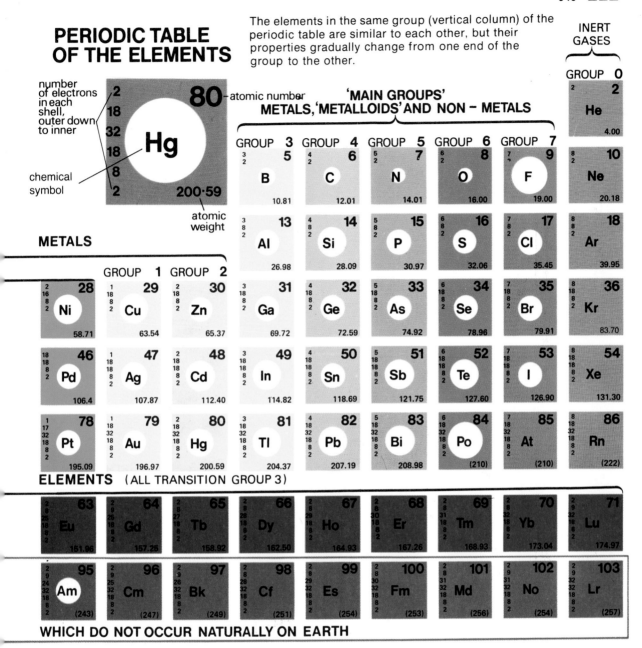

PERIODIC TABLE OF THE ELEMENTS

The elements in the same group (vertical column) of the periodic table are similar to each other, but their properties gradually change from one end of the group to the other.

INERT GASES

number of electrons in each shell, outer down to inner

80 atomic number

chemical symbol

Hg

200·59 atomic weight

'MAIN GROUPS'
METALS, 'METALLOIDS' AND NON – METALS

METALS

ELEMENTS (ALL TRANSITION GROUP 3)

WHICH DO NOT OCCUR NATURALLY ON EARTH

---

other elements. They do not have electrons to spare to link with other atoms. Helium, neon, and argon are elements with full outer shells. They do not react with other elements. They are three of the noble gases.

Elements with only a few electrons in their outer shells are more reactive. They form compounds readily with other elements. They may lend electrons to other elements, or they may share electrons with them. They may borrow electrons from other elements to fill their outer shells. These are all ways in which atoms may combine together to form compounds. (*See* VALENCE.)

The periodic table In 1869, the Russian chemist Dmitri Mendeleev drew a table of all the elements that were then known. He arranged them by their atomic weight. He showed that there was a pattern. Elements with the same sorts of properties occurred at regular intervals, or periods, in the table. Mendeleev's periodic table is still valuable. However, today we arrange the elements by atomic number, not atomic weight. We can also add a great number of elements that had not been discovered in those days.

In the table atomic numbers increase from left to right. Hydrogen, element number 1, starts the table at top left. Helium, element number 2, is at top right. The others follow in a series of rows. The horizontal rows are called periods. When they are arranged in periods like this, the elements also make vertical columns. The columns are called groups. The groups are numbered.

The elements in any particular group have similar properties. There is a gradual change, however, from top to bottom of each group. Note that groups 1 through 7 occur twice. Each occurs as a main group and as a transition group. (Main groups are sometimes given the numbers 1a, 2a, 3a, etc., and transition groups 1b, 2b, 3b, etc.) Group 8 is not divided like this. Nor is group 0, the noble gases.

The elements of main group 1a are very similar. They are all soft, light, silver-colored metals. Lithium is the lightest metal known. It is at the top of the group. It is very reactive. Further down, the metals become more reactive. Sodium (Na) reacts violently with water, and catches fire. Potassium (K) almost explodes when it touches water. Rubidium (Rb) is so reactive that it catches fire when it even meets air. It must be kept in a vacuum. Francium (Fr), at the heavy end of the group, is radioactive.

Changes like these are seen in all the groups. In main group 4a, carbon (C) is a non-metal. At the other end, tin (Sn) and lead (Pb) are metals. Between are silicon (Si) and germanium (Ge). Some have some of the properties of metals and some of the properties of non-metals. Elements like this are often called metalloids.

At the top of main group 6a is oxygen (O), which is a gas. Beneath it is sulfur (S), a non-metal solid. The other three elements are all metalloids. Polonium (Po) is highly radioactive.

The properties of the elements show an orderly pattern through main groups 1a and 7a. However, the elements in groups 3a, 4a, and 5a do not show as much resemblance among themselves as the elements in groups 1a, 2a, 6a, and 7a. In group O are the inert gases. They are almost completely unreactive, and are similar in this way.

The elements in the transition groups 1b through 7b, and group 8, are all fairly heavy metals. In group 8, the metals in the same period (horizontal row) show strong similarities. Thus iron (Fe), cobalt (Co), and nickel (Ni) are very similar metals.

Elements that show a particularly great similarity are found in transition group 3b. Elements 57 through 71 belong to the rare earth group. (*See* RARE EARTH ELEMENTS.) These are all metals. They have such similar properties that they are very difficult to separate from one another. Elements 89 through 103 show the same strong resemblance. Those after uranium (U) are artificial elements. They do not occur in nature.

Artificial elements   Artificial elements can be made from natural elements. This is done by bombarding the natural elements with subatomic particles. An atomic reactor or particle accelerator is used. Some of the artificial elements are called the transuranic elements. They are all highly radioactive and dangerous. Some, like plutonium (Pu) last for millions of years. Others, like lawrencium (Lr) decay in a matter of seconds. *See also* ACCELERATOR, PARTICLE.   D.M.H.W./J.R.W.

ELEPHANT (el′ ə fənt) The elephant is the largest living land animal. These mammals belong to the order Proboscidea, referring to their large, useful trunks. Elephants have

Indian, or Asian, elephants are smaller, less fierce and easier to tame than their African cousins. Left, an Indian elephant, ridden by his *mahout,* or driver, carries a log. Trained elephants can carry loads of up to 600 pounds on their backs or with their trunks. They are particularly useful in forestry for carrying heavy logs.

fairly large brains, weighing about 5 kg [11 lb], small eyes, and large ears. Its tusks are made of ivory and are actually incisors from the upper jaw. (See TEETH.) An elephant's trunk may be 1.8 m [6 ft] long and weigh 140 kg [308 lb]. It is boneless, contains more than 40,000 muscles, and can lift objects as small as a peanut or as large as a log weighing 275 kg [605 lb]. The tip of the trunk is very sensitive, and, like a hand, can feel an object to determine its shape, texture, and temperature.

A wild elephant eats constantly, consuming as much as 275 kg [605 lb] of food per day. The elephant, a herbivore, uses its trunk to uproot trees and plants for food. An elephant drinks by sucking water into its trunk and squirting it into its mouth.

Elephants are sometimes called pachyderms (meaning "thick-skinned") because their skin is about 2.5 cm [1 in] thick and weighs about 950 kg [2090 lb]. In spite of the thickness of the skin, elephants are very sensitive to insect bites and will leave an otherwise favorable area to avoid insects. Since the elephant lacks a protective layer of

fat under the skin, it is sensitive to very hot or very cold weather.

An elephant has large, round feet and legs which can measure 50 cm [20 in] in diameter. The feet spread out under its weight, but become smaller when lifted, keeping the elephant from getting stuck in mud or marshes. Though elephants walk at about 10 km [6 mi] per hour, a frightened elephant may run as fast as 40 km [25 mi] per hour.

A female elephant (cow) may be pregnant for 20 to 22 months before giving birth to a calf weighing about 90 kg [198 lb]. The calf nurses for three or four years, is sexually mature by age 14, and is fully grown by age 20. Most elephants live to be about 60 years old. Though many people believe that old elephants go to an "elephant graveyard" to die, this has never been proven.

Elephants are social animals, roaming in herds of 10 to 100 or more. The leader is usually a female. When elephants move from one area to another, they walk in a single file with the female leader followed by the other females, the calves, and finally, the males

Below, an African elephant with its calf. This elephant has a slow reproductive cycle, and conception to birth takes 21 months.

(bulls). If threatened, the bulls form a protective circle around the cows and calves. Adult elephants are rarely attacked by other animals, though they sometimes fight among themselves. Bulls try to gore each other with their tusks while cows try to bite off each other's tails. Rogue elephants are loners that will attack any animal or person they see. Rogues are usually old bulls that have been chased out of the herd by younger bulls. Their violent behavior is probably caused by pain from disease or decayed teeth.

There are two main species of elephants. The African elephant *(Loxodonta africana)* is dark gray, has two fingerlike structures on the tip of its trunk, and has huge ears (1.2 m [4 ft] wide). The African bull may be 3.5 m [11.5 ft] at the shoulder and weigh as much as 5,500 kg [12,100 lb]. Both bulls and cows have tusks which may be as long as 3.0 m [9.9 ft] and weigh as much as 65 kg [143 lb]. Generally, the female is smaller and has smaller tusks than the male. African elephants are found south of the Sahara Desert and north of South Africa.

The Asian (or Indian) elephant *(Elephas maximus)* is smaller and less fierce than the African elephant. It lives in India and southeast Asia. It has an arched back, two bumps on its forehead between the ears, and one fingerlike structure on the tip of its trunk. Its ears are also smaller, measuring about 0.6 m [2 ft] across. The bull stands about 2.7 m [9 ft] at the shoulder and weighs about 5,000 kg [11,000 lb]. Most Asian elephants are light gray, though some are white with pink eyes. The bull's tusks are about 1.5 m [5 ft] long, and the female's are much smaller. Some Asian elephants have no tusks at all.

Elephants have long been hunted for sport and for the valuable ivory of their tusks. Unlimited hunting has greatly reduced the numbers of elephants, and laws have been established, though rarely enforced, to protect them. In addition, refuges have been set up where hunters are not allowed to kill elephants. Unfortunately many thousands of elephants are killed illegally every year, and the wild elephant is rapidly becoming an endangered species in some areas. In other places, elephants are so numerous that control-hunting by game wardens is necessary to keep them from completely destroying the local habitat. A.J.C./J.J.M.

ELEPHANT SEAL (el′ ə fənt sēl) The elephant seal *(Mirounga leonina)*, or sea

The elephant seal is the second largest sea mammal. Only the whale is larger.

elephant, is the largest of the seals. The male (bull) may reach a length of 6 m [20 ft] and a weight of 2750 kg [6050 lb]. The female (cow) is usually about half this size. This mammal gets its name from the fact that the bull has a large nose which hangs over its mouth. This nose can be inflated to form a trunklike snout 38 cm [15 in] long.

Every year, the bulls engage in intensive fighting to establish large groups of females as mates. A cow gives birth to one calf that nurses for several weeks before joining the adults in the daily hunts for food. These seals are carnivores, feeding on squids and fishes, some of which live several hundred meters deep in the ocean.

Elephant seals have been hunted for their skins and their blubber. The blubber from one elephant seal can yield as much as 950 kg [2090 lb] of oil. Until recently, the hunting was so extensive that the elephant seal was facing extinction. Only the total prohibition of seal hunting in certain areas has allowed this species to increase its numbers beyond the endangered level. Elephant seals are found in and near Antarctica. Some have been

The head of this elephant shrew, with its large eyes and slender snout, is unlike that of the true shrew.

sighted as far north as the Pacific coast of the United States. A.J.C./J.J.M.

ELEPHANT SHREW (el′ ə fənt shrü′) The elephant shrew is any of 16 species of insect-eating mammals belonging to the family Macroscelididae. It is named for its long, flexible snout which is used to probe soil and leaf litter in search of insects. Elephant shrews vary in length from 17 to 57 cm [7 to 22 in]. They are usually yellowish in color, and have long hind legs which enable them to make great leaps if disturbed. They have large ears and eyes, and long thin tails. The elephant shrew hunts by day. It lives in dry, rocky areas of Africa. *See also* SHREW. A.J.C./J.J.M.

ELK (elk) An elk is one of two species belonging to the deer family. The American elk *(Cervus elaphus* or *Cervus canadensis)* is a brownish deer that was called *wapiti* by the American Indians. The male (bull) stands about 1.5 m [5 ft] tall at the shoulder and may weigh as much as 450 kg [990 lb]. Its antlers may spread more than 1.5 m [5 ft] and have 12 or more points. The female (cow) is smaller and does not have antlers.

American elk are herbivores and graze in large herds. They usually spend the winters in valleys where snowfall is light, returning to the mountains in the spring. Many elk die of starvation or disease in the winter. In the fall, bulls fight for mates and for leadership of the herd. Some bulls have as many as 60 cows in their groups. Pregnant females give birth to one calf in May or June.

Natural enemies of the American elk include bears, coyotes, and wolves. Elk once roamed over most of North America. Extensive hunting has now limited their range mostly to areas west of the Rocky Mountains.

The European elk *(Alces alces)* is the same species as the American moose. It is the largest European deer, measuring 2.3 m [7.6 ft] at the shoulder and weighing 820 kg [1804 lb]. The bull's antlers may have a spread of

1.8 m [6 ft]. The cow is smaller than the bull and does not have antlers. Both have coarse brown hair and white legs. The European elk is now limited to eastern Europe.

A.J.C./J.J.M.

ELM (elm) The elm is any of 18 species of large, deciduous shade trees that grow throughout North America, Europe, and Asia. The American elm *(Ulmus americana)* reaches heights of 30 m [100 ft] or more, and may live for more than 200 years. Clusters of small, greenish, bell-shaped flowers grow in the axils before the leaves appear. The flowers produce flattened fruits with wings. (*See* DIS- PERSION OF PLANTS.) These fruits are released as the lopsided, tooth-edged leaves begin to open. Since elm wood is very hard, it is a valuable source of lumber for use in making furniture, barrels, and boats. Elm wood is also a popular fuel.

There are several other important species of elms. Slippery elm *(Ulmus rubra)* has a gluey inner bark which, if chewed, gives relief to a sore throat. It was once used as a treatment for cholera. Rock or cork elm *(Ul- mus thomasii)* is known for its corky bark and its extremely hard wood. The English elm *(Ulmus procera)* is the tallest of the elms.

Elm trees are often the victims of disease. Dutch elm disease causes the most wide- spread destruction of elms. It is caused by a fungus carried by a bark beetle, and results in the death of the tree within a few weeks. Another disease, phloem necrosis, results in the death of the leaves and is caused by a virus carried by the leafhopper insect. Both of these diseases spread very rapidly, often affecting hundreds of trees before their presence is even known. Insecticides and fungicides have had limited success in controlling these diseases. There has been some success, however, in breeding an elm tree which is resistant or immune to these diseases. *See also* CLONE; HYBRID.

A.J.C./M.H.S.

EMBRYO

An embryo (em′ brē ō′) is a living thing in its earliest stages of development. An em- bryo is formed by the union of a male sex cell with a female sex cell. The sex cells are also called germ cells or gametes. Since these sex cells contain chromosomes from the parents, the embryo inherits characteristics from both parents. (*See* HEREDITY.) In plants, an em- bryo is the part of the seed that will grow into an adult. The plant embryo is formed by pol- lination, or the joining of a pollen nucleus (male sex cell) with an egg (female sex cell). In animals, an embryo is produced by fertili- zation, or the joining of a sperm (male sex cell) with an egg (female sex cell). In both plants and animals, the sex cells have half the number of chromosomes of the adult. When two sex cells join, their chromosomes add up to the number found in the adult. That is, a male sex cell with chromosome number N combines with a female sex cell with chromo- some number N to produce an embryo with chromosome number 2N, the same number as in an adult. N is used for chromosome number because different species have different num- bers of chromosomes. The chromosome number in the sex cells is half that of other cells because of a process of cellular division called meiosis.

In human beings, an embryo is formed by the joining of a sperm and an egg. During prenatal (before birth) development, a single fertilized egg cell divides and specializes into the billions of cells in the new-born baby. Once the basic body shape and organs have begun to form, usually within eight weeks, the embryo is called a fetus. At the end of a normal, nine month pregnancy, the fetus will be about 50 cm [20 in] long and weigh about 3.3 kg [7.3 lb].

Fertilization of the egg takes place in the

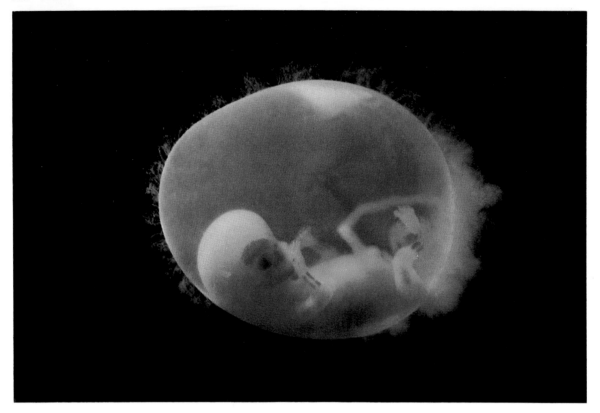

Above, a human embryo at the end of its ninth week of life, about a quarter of the way through its development. It is about 1 inch long.

woman's body in a structure called the fallopian tube. The fallopian tube is part of the female reproductive system and leads from the ovary (where the eggs are produced) to the uterus (where the baby develops). The fertilized egg is called a zygote. As the zygote moves down the fallopian tube toward the uterus, it begins to divide by mitosis. The single fertilized egg cell becomes two cells, then four cells, then eight, and so on until a small solid ball of cells called a morula is formed. This mass of cells continues dividing, forming a hollow, tennis ball-like blastula. The blastula has an inner and an outer layer of cells. In preparation for the blastula, the wall of the uterus becomes thick and rich in blood. (*See* MENSTRUAL CYCLE.) The outer layer of the blastula, the trophoblast, attaches itself to the thickened wall of the uterus, and begins the formation of a placenta and an umbilical cord. These allow oxygen and food to pass from the mother's blood to the baby's blood, and wastes to pass from the baby's blood to the mother's. It takes about two months for the placenta and umbilical cord to be fully developed.

The inner layer of the blastula, the embryoblast, develops into an embryonic disk. The embryonic disk develops into a tube-shaped gastrula with three layers of cells, the outer ectoderm, the inner endoderm, and the middle mesoderm. Each of these layers produces specific structures in the adult. The ectoderm develops into the skin, hair, nails, brain, nervous sytem, part of the eye, and part of the ear. The endoderm produces most of the alimentary canal and its associated organs. It also produces the tissue which lines or surrounds internal organs. The mesoderm develops into most of the internal tissues and organs, such as the heart, kidneys, muscles, bones, and blood.

The development of all of these structures is the result of cellular differentiation. The

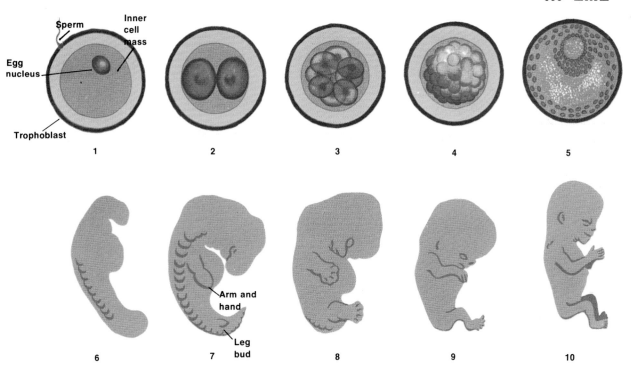

Some stages in the development of the human embryo. 1. A sperm fertilizes the egg. 2. The nucleus of the fertilized egg divides in two. 3. Each cell has divided twice to produce eight. 4. Further divisions produce a blackberrylike mass. 5. The cell mass divides into an outer sphere and an inner cell mass from which the embryo grows. 6. The embryo at 3 1/2 weeks shows the beginnings of the backbone. 7. At 6 weeks the arms have appeared, as well as budlike legs. 8. At 7 weeks growth of the brain increases. 9. At 8 weeks the limbs are recognizably formed. 10. At 12 weeks the embryo is a recognizable baby.

process involved is not clearly understood, but cells specialize to perform certain functions in specific tissues or organs. After about four weeks, the embryo is about 6 mm [0.25 in] long. The head is large and bent over. There are small swellings called buds on the side of the embryo. These buds will develop into arms and legs. There are blocks of tissue called somites arranged along the embryo's body. These somites develop into bones and muscles. Within eight weeks after fertilization, cellular differentiation is virtually complete and the embryo is about 25 mm [1 in] long. These first eight weeks are the most important in the development of the child because it is during this time that all the adult structures are established and begin to grow. At eight weeks, the fetus can be recognized as being human, with human features and structures.

Birth defects, though relatively rare, are usually a result of some malfunction during these first two months. The malfunction may be caused by faulty chromosomes from one or both parents, or by external reasons such as radiation, certain drugs, or certain diseases. (*See* MUTATION.) *See also* GESTATION PERIOD; REPRODUCTION.   A.J.C./E.R.L.

EMERALD (em′ rəld) Emerald, a rich green gemstone, is a variety of the mineral beryl. The highest quality emeralds come from Columbia. Columbia is also the largest producer of these gems. Emeralds are also mined in India, Rhodesia, Russia, and North Carolina.

A natural emerald crystal has a six-sided form. Large and perfect emeralds are about equal in value to diamonds. One of the largest emeralds known to exist is displayed in a museum in Russia. This emerald weighs about 2.7 kg [6 lbs]. The oriental emerald is a form of the mineral corundum, not beryl as the name would indicate.　　　　J.J.A./R.H.

A natural emerald crystal has a six-sided form. All emeralds except Oriental emeralds are forms of the mineral beryl.

EMERY (em′ rē) Emery, a dull gray material, is a variety of the mineral corundum. Emery is mined chiefly in Russia and the United States.

Emery is used to grind metals, gems, and optical lenses. Emery is first crushed into tiny pieces or a fine powder. It may then be mounted on paper or mixed with cement and formed into grinding wheels. Manufactured abrasives, such as aluminum oxide and silicon carbide, have largely replaced emery.

J.J.A./R.H.

EMOTION (i mō′ shən) Emotion is a reaction involving a strong feeling or feelings. Common emotions include joy, love, hope, desire, fear, anger, hate, and sadness. Emotional reactions can be aroused by thoughts or outside events.

A child is born with emotional reactions to only a few things, such as pain and hunger. However, he soon learns to respond emotion-ally to other things. For example, when a child first meets a snarling dog, the child may have no emotion toward the dog. But if the dog tries to bite the child, the child develops fear toward the dog. Having learned the fear of snarling dogs, the child avoids them in the future.

Emotional responses are an important form of self-defense. They result in bodily changes that help to give protection against danger. For example, the adrenal glands pour the hormone adrenaline into the bloodstream when a person is afraid. This increases the rate of the heartbeat and the depth of breathing, and releases emergency food supplies for use by the muscles. All these help the person to meet the danger or flee from it.

Emotional responses may also be harmful. If the body changes caused by emotions continue for a long time, vital tissue damage can result. For example, constant fear can produce stomach ulcers. Strong emotions can make it hard to think and to solve problems. A student taking a test may be so worried about failing that he or she cannot think properly. The worry drains mental energy needed for the test. *See also* PSYCHOSOMATIC DISORDER.

J.J.A./J.J.F.

EMULSION (i məl′ shən) Emulsion is a preparation of one liquid dispersed, or evenly distributed, in another. The two liquids do not dissolve in each other. Tiny drops of the dispersed liquid remain suspended in the other liquid. (*See* COLLOID.)

Emulsions are not stable. The liquids usually separate from each other after a certain time. An emulsifying agent, such as soap, may be needed to stabilize the emulsion and prevent it from separating.

Common substances such as cosmetic lotions, foods, lubricants, medicines, and paints are emulsions.

Oil and water form the most common emulsions. An emulsion can be formed by either droplets of oil dispersed in water or droplets of water in oil. For example, milk is an emulsion of butterfat in water. The emulsifying agent that keeps butterfat suspended in milk is the protein casein. *See also* SUSPENSION.   J.J.A./A.D.

ENAMEL (in am′ əl) Enamel is a glasslike substance applied as a coating to metal and ceramic objects. It is produced in many colors. Enamel is commonly used as a protective surface for such things as cooking utensils, and kitchen and bathroom fixtures.

An enamel coating is applied to an object by first grinding sand, borax, and metallic compounds into a fine mixture of particles. This mixture is applied to the object to be enameled by melting (firing) the mixture onto the metal. The heat melts the enamel and combines it with the surface of the article.

There are several types of decorative enameling. Cloisonné or celled enamel is made by bending and soldering metal strips together to make a design. The holes in the design are filled with different colored mixtures and the object is fired. The heat melts the enamel to bind it with the metal. Champlevé or inlaid enamel is made by filling designs engraved in metal with enamel.

                                        J.M.C./A.D.

ENDOCRINE (en′ də krən) The term "endocrine" refers to a type of gland. An endocrine gland is a group of cells that have special functions in regulating the body.

Glands make chemical substances. Those glands that send out their secretions directly to the body tissues through ducts are called exocrine. Examples of the exocrine glands include the salivary glands, which produce saliva in the mouth; lachrymal, or tear glands; and sweat glands.

The endocrine glands secrete their hormones directly into the blood stream, without passing through a duct. They are located in various parts of the body. Each gland has one or more specific jobs to do. For example, the

pituitary gland is located at the base of the brain. It is called the "master" endocrine gland because it controls the action of some of the other glands. Other endocrine glands include the thyroid gland, the adrenal glands, the pineal, and the pancreas.

The endocrine glands are very important. If one of them is not working the way it should, serious disease or death can result. The endocrine gland system is very complicated. It has been studied extensively by medical specialists, called endocrinologists.

                                        P.G.C./J.J.F.

ENDOSPERM (en′ də spərm′) An endosperm is a food-storing tissue that surrounds and nourishes the embryo in a seed. In some seeds, such as the bean and the pea, the endosperm is completely absorbed before the seed matures. In others, such as wheat, part of the endosperm remains until the seed germinates. (*See* GERMINATION.) It is the endosperm that provides most of the edible material in cereal crops and in oil-producing seeds, such as corn. The coconut has a liquid endosperm, the coconut milk.

In angiosperms, the endosperm contains three sets of chromosomes instead of the usual two. This condition (3N) results from the fusion, or joining, of one pollen nucleus (N) with two polar bodies (N, N) in the ovary of the pistil. Polar bodies are produced as "side products" when an egg divides by meiosis. *See also* CHROMOSOME; GAMETE.

                                        A.J.C./M.H.S.

ENDOSPORE (en′ də spōr′) An endospore is a thick-walled cell which is well-suited for dormancy and can tolerate many unfavorable environmental conditions. Endospores are an important part of asexual reproduction in certain algae and fungi.

Some bacteria, usually the rod-shaped bacilli, produce endospores which may be dormant for years. These endospores can withstand extreme conditions, such as boiling or freezing, without damage. When conditions become favorable, the endospores develop into bacteria. Endospores are a major cause of food poisoning in improperly processed foods. Fortunately, few pathogenic (disease-causing) bacteria produce endospores. *See also* BOTULISM; FOOD PRESERVATION.   A.J.C./M.H.S.

ENDOTHERMIC REACTION (en' də thər' mik rē ak' shən) An endothermic reaction is a chemical reaction that absorbs heat. Endothermic reactions are important in the cooling of food. For example, if several ice cubes are placed in a warm drink, the ice absorbs heat as it melts. Eventually, if there is enough ice, the temperature of the drink drops to the temperature of the ice cubes, 0°C [32°F].

A chemical reaction that gives off heat is called an exothermic reaction.   J.M.C./A.D.

ENERGY

If anything can do work, then it is said to possess energy (en' ər jē). To carry out any task, we need to perform work. Machines are capable of doing work. Work is required to dig a garden or to saw a block of wood, for example.

There are many different kinds of energy. All living things need energy to grow. Plants get energy from the light of the sun. This is electromagnetic energy. (*See* PHOTOSYNTHESIS.) Plants also feed through their roots and get energy from the nutrients thus acquired. Heat and light are both forms of energy. Animals get their energy by eating plants and other animals. The food is digested and provides a source of chemical energy for the animal. We need energy to heat our

Different forms of energy. 1. Water stored in a dam illustrates potential energy. 2. Motion is a form of kinetic energy. 3. An atomic reactor harnesses nuclear energy. 4. The panels on this satellite collect solar energy. 5. Power lines carry electrical energy from one place to another. 6. A burning fire is an example of chemical energy.

houses. This energy is often provided by burning fuels, such as coal or gas. Fuels contain chemical energy. When they are burned, the chemical energy is turned into heat energy. This is one example of energy conversion. Most forms of energy can be converted into other forms. Energy conversion is often used to convert one form of energy into another, more useful, form.

If an object is moving, the energy of its movement is called kinetic energy. When you run, the fact that you are moving means that you possess kinetic energy. This energy comes from the chemical energy of the food that you eat. Another kind of energy is called potential energy. This is stored energy. When you wind up a clock you are converting the kinetic energy of the turning key into potential energy. This potential energy is stored either in the tightly wound spring or in the weights of a pendulum clock. When you wind up a pendulum clock you raise the weights. As the weights slowly fall under gravity their potential energy is converted back into the kinetic energy of the moving gears, levers, and hands.

The water behind a dam also has potential energy. If the dam were to break, the water would rush down the valley. The potential energy would have been converted into the kinetic energy of the moving water. The potential energy of the water can be used to produce electricity. The water flows through a turbine and causes its blades to rotate. The potential energy of the water behind the dam is converted to the kinetic energy of moving water, which is then turned into the kinetic energy of the blades. A generator then converts the kinetic energy into electrical energy. (*See* GENERATOR; HYDROELECTRIC POWER.)

Albert Einstein was one of the greatest physicists of all time. (*See* EINSTEIN, ALBERT.) He was the first person to show that mass is equivalent to energy. A mass of one kilogram converts to the amount of energy a large power station produces in three years.

One might think that the mass of a nucleus would be the same as the mass of its protons and neutrons. In fact, the mass of the nucleus is a little smaller. When protons and neutrons form a nucleus, some of their mass disappears. It is converted into nuclear energy to bind these particles together.

A nuclear power station converts some of this nuclear energy into electrical energy. Nuclear energy can also be used destructively, as in a nuclear weapon. Stars contain huge amounts of energy. We see some of this energy as light. This energy comes from nuclear energy. Stars ''burn'' their mass into energy.

Conservation of energy One form of energy can change into another. But if the mass of the system does not change, the total amount of energy always remains the same. This is the law of the conservation of energy. For example, when 3.8 liters [1 gallon] of gasoline is burned in a car engine, about 100,000 kilojoules of chemical energy are converted into heat energy. Although only about 25,000 kJ (kilojoules) are actually used in driving the car, the remaining 75,000 kJ do not disappear. They are wasted by heating up the engine's cooling water and heating up the air with the exhaust gases. Some energy, too, is used in overcoming the friction forces in the engine. But you could do a sum to show that the heat energy produced by the fuel is equal to the energy used in driving the car added to the energy wasted in heating up the surroundings.

If nuclear energy is involved in the energy change, the change in the mass of the fuel has to be taken into account. Then the law of the conservation of energy becomes the law of the conservation of mass and energy. In this case the energy produced during a day is equal to the loss in the mass of the fuel during the day.

Energy supplies The economic law of supply and demand applies to energy as well as to

The solar photograph (facing left) shows an eruption on the sun's surface.

goods and services. The price we pay for something is influenced by what happens to the supply or demand for it. When oil is in short supply, the price of its by-products— gasoline, for example—will rise. So would the price of the oil and gas we use to heat our homes and factories. Oil and gas are natural sources of energy. They come from fossil fuels that were stored in the earth millions of years ago. This supply is limited and is running out.

Once again, coal is claiming the attention of business and industry. This fossil fuel exists in great abundance. But it fell into disfavor when oil and natural gas became more available. Electricity also helped to displace coal as an energy source. All of these newer energy sources are clean. They do not pollute the air as burning coal does. If this drawback of coal could be solved, our energy supply would be assured for many years. The application of total automation to mining and processing could get coal out of the ground in sufficient quantity to meet the energy demands of our growing population. But this will take time.

Meanwhile, other sources of energy might help solve the problem of supply. Nuclear energy is a possible solution. But nuclear processes produce large quantities of dangerous wastes. And many people are afraid to live near, or work in, nuclear-powered industries that might accidentally emit radiation. A safer source would be the geothermal energy that lies deep in the earth. This heat energy comes to the surface as geysers and volcanic

The wind turbine (right) can, in a 13 kilometer-per-hour [8 mph] wind, produce enough energy to be used by fifty average homes.

eruptions. Some geothermal sources are hot enough to be of practical use in turning turbines that generate electricity. Geothermal power already is serving the needs of more than a million people in one part of California. But a disadvantage of tapping geothermal energy sources is its possible destructive effect on the environment.

Another likely source is thermonuclear reactions. Such reactions occur in the sun and other stars. With increased understanding of them, scientists hope to find an application on earth. This method would supply us with huge amounts of energy. But many technical problems are involved. However, much progress has been made in utilizing the radiant energy of the sun directly. Solar heating of homes and other buildings is gaining acceptance. And solar cells and solar batteries for converting radiant energy to electricity are finding other than space flight uses.

Still another possibility lies in the kinetic energy of tides. Some countries are already using this energy source but only on a small scale. In America, the windmill is making a comeback—mostly as a turbine for generating electricity. M.E./J.T.

ENGINE

An engine (en' jǝn) is a device that uses the energy in a fuel to do work. The energy in the chemicals of the fuel is first turned into heat energy. The heat is then used to move the metal parts of a machine. There are many kinds of fuel. Most engines use gasoline, oil, kerosene, coal, or coke. The heat that comes from burning the fuel makes a gas expand. This expanded gas drives pistons or turbine blades. The pistons or turbines turn shafts. The turning shafts move gears and other wheels. We use these rotating wheels and shafts to move automobiles, airplanes, and other transport. We can also use them for pumping, drilling, digging, and other such activities.

Early engines burned coal or wood to heat water. The steam was used to drive steam engines. Until the middle of this century, most locomotives were powered by steam. At the beginning of the century, even some automobiles were run on steam. We still use steam engines, but most of them are being replaced by more efficient engines. Today we have powerful gasoline and diesel engines to work for us.

The gasoline engine The engines of most automobiles and small vehicles use gasoline as fuel. The gasoline engine is an internal-combustion engine. The fuel is burned in combustion (burning) chambers inside the engine. The combustion chambers are placed at one end of the cylinders. Pistons move up and down in the cylinders. They are pushed by the hot gases from the burning fuel. When the fuel is mixed with air it burns so quickly that it explodes. The combustion chambers and cylinders are made strong enough not to break during the explosion. Instead of blowing the cylinder apart like a bomb, the explosion simply kicks hard against the head of the piston. It pushes it as far as it can.

Each movement of a piston up or down in its cylinder is called a stroke. Most gasoline engines work on a four-stroke cycle. This means that each piston goes up and down twice for each explosion. That makes four movements or strokes. This cycle of events is repeated over and over again. On the first downstroke, the piston moves to the lowest part of the cylinder. A mixture of gasoline droplets and air is drawn into the cylinder above it. Now the piston moves up again. This is its second stroke. It squeezes the mixture into a small space. An electric spark lights the mixture, and it explodes. The piston is forced down again for its third stroke. This is called the power stroke. For the fourth stroke, the piston moves to the top again. This time·it pushes the burnt gases out of the cylinder. The gases leave the engine as exhaust fumes.

The first engine that used the four-stroke cycle was made in about 1876. It was designed by the German engineer, Nikolaus August Otto. He used coal gas, not gasoline. The first engines to burn gasoline were developed by Karl Benz and Gottlieb Daimler. These two men were famous as automobile pioneers. (*See* AUTOMOBILE.)

A piston simply going up and down cannot push an automobile along. Its movement must be changed to a turning movement. To do this, a crankshaft is used. Each piston of the engine is linked to part of the crankshaft. Each push it gives makes the shaft turn. The spinning shaft passes the power on to the automobile's transmission system. It usually does this through a heavy flywheel. The transmission system transmits power to the clutch and to the propeller shaft, through a gearbox. The propeller shaft drives the road wheels by means of axles.

To keep an automobile engine going, there need to be several systems. There must be a fuel system. This has to supply gasoline to the engine cylinders in the right amounts. It has also to mix it with the right amount of air, so that it will explode properly. There must be an ignition system. This has to provide sparks to ignite the explosive mixture at exactly the right time. There has to be a cooling system, otherwise the engine would overheat. The lubrication system must keep all the moving parts oiled and moving freely. Too much friction causes wear of the metal and makes the engine overheat.

The engine unit The gasoline engine has two basic parts. They are called the cylinder head and the cylinder block. The cylinder block is machined from solid metal. The metal is usually cast iron. Sometimes aluminum is used because it is much lighter. It also carries heat away quickly. Inside the cylinder block are the cylinders. The walls of the cylinders have to be very accurately made, and are highly polished. The pistons that move up and down in the cylinders must be accurately made, too. They have springy bands of metal around them to press tight against the cylinder walls and stop gases leaking. The bands are called piston rings. They are often made of aluminum alloy for strength and lightness.

An engine may have any number of cylinders. They may be arranged in a line, or in opposite pairs. If they are in pairs, they are often arranged in a "V" shape. In many airplanes with piston engines, the cylinders are arranged in a ring around the crankshaft.

The lower part of the cylinder block is called the crankcase. This is where the crankshaft lies. The crankshaft is linked to each piston by a connecting rod. The crankshaft is made in a single piece. It must be tough and accurately machined. It may spin as many as 6,000 times a minute. It changes the up-and-down motion of the piston into a turning motion. It does this by means of cranks, one for each piston. The cranks are set at different angles round the shaft. Each piston gives a push to its crank during its power stroke. During the other three strokes, the crank pushes the piston up, down and up again. The heavy flywheel is bolted to one end of the crankshaft. It keeps the shaft turning smoothly between the power strokes. Strong main bearings support the crankshaft in its case.

The cylinder head is bolted to the cylinder block. Inside it are the combustion chambers. Each combustion chamber is a space above a piston inside a cylinder. This is where the explosion of the mixture of fuel and air takes place. A spark plug is set into the top of the chamber. Each chamber has a pair of valves. There is an inlet valve to allow the fuel and air mixture into the chamber. The other valve is an outlet or exhaust valve. Through this pass the burnt gases after the explosion. The valves are opened and closed by push rods and springs. The push rods are moved up and down by links with the crankshaft. The linkage is through a turning shaft called the camshaft.

To carry water to cool the engine, there are passages in the metal of the cylinder head and cylinder block. Oil passes through other passages. Between the cylinder head and block is a gasket. This is a thin plate of metal that acts as a seal. It is put in when the parts of the engine are bolted together. It is often made of copper.

The fuel system The fuel system of the engine supplies the gasoline to be burnt. The gasoline is stored in a large tank. In a powerful car, the tank holds many gallons of fuel. The tank is placed well away from the engine, to reduce the risk of fire. The gasoline is pumped through a fuel line. The pump may be driven by links with the engine camshaft. Sometimes it has its own electric motor. Before the gasoline reaches the cylinders, it must be mixed with air. The fuel line leads to the carburetor. In the carburetor the gasoline is forced through a fine nozzle, or jet. It forms a spray of small droplets. The droplets vaporize as they mix with the air. Now the mixture is ready for ignition.

The speed of the engine is controlled by a throttle valve. Opening and closing the throttle valve regulates the amount of mixture leaving the carburetor. From the carburetor the mixture passes to the inlet valves of the combustion chambers. The mixture is delivered through a set of tubes called the inlet manifold. A similar set of tubes takes away exhaust gases from the exhaust valves of the combustion chambers. This is called the exhaust manifold. It leads to the outside air through the exhaust pipe. The exhaust pipe is fitted with a muffler, or silencer, to reduce noise.

In some automobiles, the fuel is delivered by a different system. Instead of passing through a carburetor, the fuel is sprayed into the airstream just before the inlet valves. It is sprayed in small amounts, which are carefully metered. The system is called fuel injection.

The ignition system The mixture inside each cylinder must be made to explode. A spark is used to do this. The spark must jump across the gap in the spark plug at exactly the right time. Each of the automobile's cylinders must fire in turn. The ignition system depends upon very accurate timing. If the sparks are a fraction of a second too early or too late, the engine will not run properly.

The electricity to make the sparks comes from the automobile's electric storage battery. This battery is kept charged by a dynamo, or generator, run by the engine. The battery supplies electricity at only about 12 volts. To make a spark, thousands of volts are required. The voltage from the battery is boosted up to about 30,000 volts by means of a transformer. The transformer is called the ignition coil. The ignition coil supplies high voltage to the distributor. This is a device that "distributes" electricity in surges, or pulses, to each of the spark plugs in turn. When a surge of electricity at high voltage reaches a plug, a spark leaps across a small gap. The spark is so hot that it makes the mixture of gasoline and air ignite and explode.

The cooling system The heat produced by burning the gasoline in the engine is very great. The temperature inside each combustion chamber may reach more than 1,000°C [over 1,800°F]. The engine must be constantly cooled. The cooling system supplies cool water through channels called water jackets. The water jackets surround the cylinders. They carry away the excess heat as the water passes through them. The hot water is led away to be cooled in the radiator. The radiator is a system of many tubes, linked together, with spaces between them. Cold air from the front of the autuombile rushes between the tubes. A fan, driven by the engine,

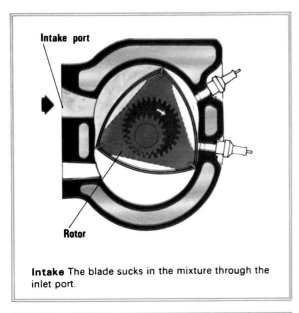

Intake The blade sucks in the mixture through the inlet port.

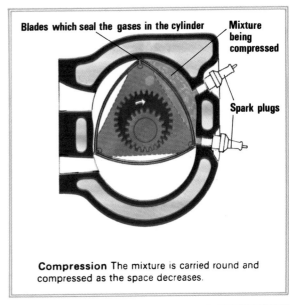

Compression The mixture is carried round and compressed as the space decreases.

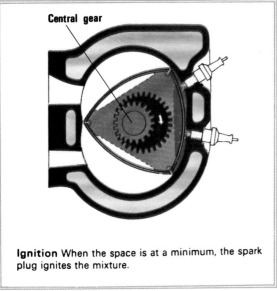

Ignition When the space is at a minimum, the spark plug ignites the mixture.

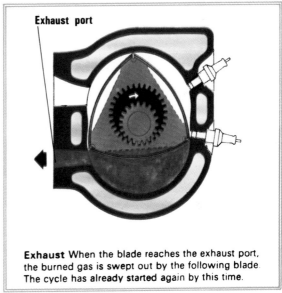

Exhaust When the blade reaches the exhaust port, the burned gas is swept out by the following blade. The cycle has already started again by this time.

The illustrations above show the sequence of events in the workings of a Wankel engine.

speeds up the flow of air. The hot water loses its heat to the air. The cooled water is then pumped to the engine again.

Some automobiles do not have a water-cooled system. They use air cooling. Air from the front of the automobile is blown over the cylinder block and the cylinder head. The engine is fitted with special cooling fins, sticking out into the airstream. These help the heat to radiate more quickly. Air-cooled engines tend to be noisier than water-cooled engines.

In a water-cooled engine, the water jacket helps to absorb the engine noise.

To prevent the water in the cooling system from freezing in cold weather, antifreeze is usually added in winter. This is often ethylene glycol or a similar compound.

The lubrication system Oil is needed to keep the engine's parts from wearing too quickly. A storage tank of oil, called the sump, is attached under the crankcase. The oil is pumped through channels to all the main bearings and the big-end bearings. Eventually it reaches the sump again. It passes through a filter to remove dirt before it is used again. Whenever metal surfaces rub against others, tiny particles are worn off. The oil picks them up as it flows between the surfaces. They are trapped by the oil filter. The filter must be changed regularly. The oil itself gradually burns and becomes impure. It must be replaced at intervals.

The Wankel engine   The Wankel engine is a gasoline engine that works without pistons. It was invented in Germany by Felix Wankel. He started development of it in 1956. The pistons in an ordinary gasoline engine must move up and down, or backwards and forwards. This kind of motion is called reciprocating motion. It needs to be converted into a turning motion (rotary motion) by a crankshaft. In a Wankel engine, burning the fuel produces a rotary motion directly. There is no need for a crankshaft. It is a rotary engine.

A Wankel engine has a specially designed combustion chamber. It is roughly an ellipse, or oval, in shape. Inside is a rotor. The rotor is shaped like a triangle with bulging, rounded sides. Through the center of the rotor passes the driving shaft. It has teeth like a gearwheel that meet teeth inside the rotor. The rotor is shaped so that its corners just touch the walls of the chamber. The rotor can move up and down and also side to side as it turns.

The rotor divides the chamber into three parts. As the rotor turns, the shapes of the three parts change. They act like three separate combustion chambers. As in an ordinary engine, there are spark plugs, an inlet port for the gasoline and air mixture, and an outlet port for the exhaust gases.

The rotor turns so that each part of the chamber in turn meets the inlet. The gasoline and air mixture is drawn in. This is like the first piston downstroke of an ordinary engine. Further turning sweeps the mixture round into a smaller space. The mixture is compressed.

This is like the second stroke. Now the spark plug fires. The explosion drives the rotor further around. This is the power stroke. When the rotor has turned a little further, the exhaust gases are pushed from the chamber through the exhaust port. The process is continuous. It happens as each part of the chamber sweeps round.

The Wankel engine has several advantages over an ordinary engine. It has fewer moving parts. There is less vibration. It is lighter. It costs less to produce. However, there are difficulties. The main difficulty is ensuring that the seals, where the corners of the rotor meet the chamber walls, are gastight. The Wankel engine is used successfully in several kinds of automobile. *See also:* DIESEL; JET PROPULSION; SOLAR ENERGY.

D.W./J.T.

ENGINEERING (en′ jə nir′ ing) Engineering deals with the ways in which we use natural materials for our own purposes. It covers a very wide field. It deals with everything from designing a new rocket to building huge skyscrapers. Some engineers specialize in electrical equipment. Others make a special study of plastics. Others are experts in building safe bridges. There are many specializations. But all engineers have one thing in common. They put scientific knowledge to practical use.

A few hundred years ago, there were only two divisions of engineering. Military engineering dealt with weapons and engines for warfare. Military engineers built roads for soldiers to use, and fortified walls and ditches for defense. The Roman armies had expert engineers. Some great scientists, such as Leonardo da Vinci, put their minds to military problems. Civil engineering dealt with the building of roads, bridges, canals, and aqueducts for towns and cities. Early civil engineers designed irrigation systems for the

The three engineers (facing right) are examining the blueprints of a building project.

countryside. This made it possible for agriculture to support city life. Some of the roads, bridges, sewers, and canals built hundreds of years ago are still in use today.

The greatest advances in engineering have been in the last 200 years. During these centuries scientific knowledge has grown very rapidly. Engineers have become specialists in particular fields. Today we can divide engineering into five main branches. These are: civil, mechanical, mining and metallurgical, chemical, and electrical engineering.

Civil engineering   Civil engineering is the design and building of roads, bridges, waterways, airports, canals, dams, sewers, railroads, hospitals, and other public buildings. Safety is most important in all construction of this kind. Engineers must study soils and rocks so that they can decide the correct foundations to build. They must know the strengths of all the materials they use. They must know the maximum load that is safe for bridges. They have to know how much water a dam can safely hold.

Architects and civil engineers work closely together. An architect is responsible for producing a pleasing and efficient design. It is the civil engineer's job to check that suitable materials are used to build a structure. It is no use having a good-looking bridge that is unsafe. Teams of experts work together on big projects.

Civil engineers also have to know about the equipment that is used in building. They have to decide how to move materials, using cranes, bulldozers, mechanical shovels, and other vehicles. They give advice about everything from welding girders to using a pile-driver. Civil engineering is one of the biggest branches of engineering. It covers many specialities.

Mechanical engineering   Mechanical engineers are the experts in machinery. They are concerned with using energy to produce mechanical power. Every industry you can think of uses machines of some kind. The farmer uses tractors, seed-drills and sprayers. In a plastics factory there are hundreds of machines, for melting, mixing, molding, rolling, and stamping. New machinery is in demand all the time. It is the job of mechanical engineers to design and construct machines.

In the power-producing industries, specialized machinery is needed. Different kinds of machinery and equipment are used to produce power from natural resources. Mechanical engineers have to deal with coal, natural gas, oil, and other fuels in power-producing plants. Nuclear fuels require machinery of a different kind.

Aeronautical engineering is a specialized kind of engineering dealing with aircraft. Automotive engineering deals with the design and building of automobiles. Marine engineering deals not only with ships and submarines, but with docks and other equipment. There are numerous other specialities in mechanical engineering.

Mining and metallurgical engineering   This deals with the ways that ores and minerals can be discovered and brought up from the earth. It also deals with the ways that metals can be extracted from their ores and prepared for use. A mining engineer work closely with geologists, who study the rock in the earth.

Mining engineers must know the best way to construct mine shafts in different circumstances. They must know about machinery to ventilate the shafts. They must know about drills and digging equipment to extract minerals from the earth. Mining engineers may specialize in coal mining, uranium mining, gold mining, or another field. They need a sound knowledge of civil, mechanical, and electrical engineering.

Metallurgical engineers are experts in separating minerals from their ores and preparing them for use. Another name for metallurgical engineer is extractive metallurgist. He or she deals with how to get the metal iron from different kinds of iron ore. A physical metallurgist tests minerals and metals for strength and hardness.

Chemical engineering   Chemical engineering deals with the ways raw materials can be changed into useful products. A chemical engineer may be a specialist in one chemical process. He or she may specialize in making paint, dyes, fertilizers, plastics, soaps, explosives, drugs, or one of hundreds of other things. The chemical engineer must understand how to handle large quantities of chemicals. Some chemicals are very dangerous. To handle them safely needs an expert knowledge. Some chemicals may need special equipment to transport them. This is the chemical engineer's job.

There are numerous different processes for which chemical engineers may be responsible. Some of them are distillation, crystallization, filtration, mixing, crushing, and drying of chemical compounds.

Electrical engineering   Electrical engineering deals with the construction and use of different kinds of electrical equipment. Electrical equipment is used in power plants, radio and television stations, radar, telephones, and air-conditioning systems.

Electricity generators may be run by water power, nuclear power, or coal or oil. There are many specialist electrical engineers. Electronics engineers design and build miniature electronic circuits. Communications engineers are experts in radio, television, radar, and telephones.   D.M.H.W./R.W.L.

ENTOMOLOGY (ent′ ə mäl′ ə jē) Entomology is the study of insects. This vast group includes three-fourths of the known animal species. Entomologists (scientists who study insects) study the anatomy, physiology, behavior, ecology, and classi-fication of insects. The field of entomology often also includes organisms closely related to insects, like spiders and centipedes.

Many entomologists study the effects that insects have on human life. For example, medical entomologists study insects that carry diseases, like the mosquitos. Some entomologists study the effect of insects on farm crops, while others study certain insects called parasites that live off other organisms. Scientists often develop insecticides to kill harmful insects if they discover how and why an insect's body works. Harmful insects are now often deliberately controlled by other means, such as by using insects' parasites or diseases or by sterilizing the males so they can not produce offspring.

Entomology helps people to understand the function of insects in the ecosystems of the earth. Today, entomologists realize that most insects are beneficial or harmless to humans and their crops and animals.   J.M.C./J.R.

ENTROPY (en′ trə pē) Entropy is a measure of the internal disorder of matter. At a temperature of absolute zero, all the atoms and molecules of a crystal stop moving and are held in fixed positions. At such a time, there is no disorder. The atoms in a diamond crystal, at room temperature, are held by chemical bonds in a rigid framework. The only movement is the vibration of the atoms. But a few of the atoms escape from the framework and there is a small amount of disorder, or entropy. Atoms of helium gas in a balloon are very disordered. They move about within the balloon, colliding with each other and with the walls of the balloon. Helium gas has a higher entropy than a diamond.

Entropy is a very useful idea in some heat calculations. (*See* THERMODYNAMICS.) It is also used in information theory to describe how well a system can handle information. A system that has a high degree of unpredictability has high entropy. *See also* ABSOLUTE ZERO; BOND, CHEMICAL.   W.R.P./A.I.

Above, the Eastern Highlands of New Guinea are a natural environment largely undisturbed by the growth of industrial civilization.

ENVIRONMENT (in vī' rən mənt) Every organism is affected by many outside influences. These influences include: soil, air, water, temperature, chemicals, amount of sunlight, wind, and many other things. These influences are commonly referred to as environmental conditions. The total of all environmental conditions acting upon an organism is its environment.

There are many different environments. The environment of a forest is often well-shaded, cool, and moist. The desert environment is usually hot and dry. The environment at the bottom of the ocean is cold and dark, with a tremendous amount of pressure. The environment of a place will determine what organisms can live at that place. An oak tree will not grow at the bottom of an ocean, nor will a fish live on desert sands. Often, organisms are able to change an environment. (*See* SUCCESSION.)

Humans are able to change environments more than any other organism. They can move mountains, dam rivers, drain lakes, and even make it rain. By changing the environment around them, humans have been able to make life more comfortable. They may now live anywhere they choose. (*See* ADAPTATION.) People can also do great harm to the earth by changing environments. They have caused floods, droughts, the extinction of animals, the spread of diseases, and the spoiling of air and water. (*See* POLLUTION.) We now realize that we must not make great changes in our environment because it is impossible to do just one thing to the environment. If we do one thing, many other unplanned things may also result. *See also* CONSERVATION; ECOLOGY; ECOSYSTEM; POLLUTION. S.R.G./R.J.B.

ENZYME (en' zīm') Enzymes are proteins made in the cells of plants and animals. They cause or speed up chemical reactions. The millions of chemical reactions that make up the metabolism of an organism are controlled by enzymes.

Unlike most chemical reactions, an enzyme-controlled reaction occurs at about the body temperature of an organism—about 37°C [98.6°F] in humans. A chemical reaction that requires high temperature to occur outside the body, like the breakdown of sugar, occurs at the body temperature when it is enzyme-controlled. The body breaks down sugar in a rapid series of enzyme-controlled reactions that release energy slowly. In this way, the body benefits as much as possible from each chemical reaction.

Enzymes are very sensitive substances and may become inactive at high temperature. If a person's body temperature rises to 42°C [108°F], many enzymes stop working, and death becomes a possibility.

An enzyme works by attaching itself to another chemical substance called a substrate. The substrate-enzyme complex goes through the chemical reaction, after which it is released unchanged. Some enzymes need an additional substance to allow attachment to the substrate. These substances are called co-enzymes. Many vitamins are co-enzymes.

Some methods of chemical and biological warfare use poisons that combine with enzymes so as to inactivate them. If enough enzymes are blocked, death may occur. *See also* BIOCHEMISTRY. J.M.C./J.M.

EOCENE EPOCH (ē′ ə sēn′ ep′ ək) The Eocene epoch is the part of the Tertiary period which started about 55 million years ago and lasted about 15 million years. Mammals were well established by this time. Small ancestors of the horse and camel appeared. Primitive whales and rodents developed during this epoch.

Many modern plants lived during the Eocene epoch, including fruits, flowering plants, and grasses. *See also* GEOLOGICAL TIME SCALE.   J.M.C./W.R.S.

EPHEMERAL PLANT (i fem′ rəl plant) An ephemeral plant is one which lives for only a short time. Weeds and some other plants produce seeds which germinate, grow, flower, produce new seeds, and die, all within a few weeks. Most ephemeral plants produce one or more generations each year. The seeds of some ephemeral plants are coated with a chemical inhibitor which prevents growth. This chemical must be washed off by heavy rainfall before the seed will germinate. In this way, the seed remains dormant until there is enough water to support growth. (*See* DORMANCY.)   A.J.C./M.H.S.

EPIDEMIC (ep′ ə dem′ ik) An epidemic is the widespread outbreak of a disease. If it is a serious disease, an epidemic may kill thousands of people. In the fourteenth century, the Black Death, an epidemic of bubonic plague, swept across Europe and killed one quarter of the population. A worldwide epidemic is called a pandemic. J.M.C./J.J.F.

EPILEPSY (ep′ ə lep′ sē) Epilepsy is a disturbance of the activity of certain cells in the brain. People with epilepsy have attacks or seizures. The seizure occurs when the nerve cells controlling muscular activity do not operate properly. There are three types of seizures: grand mal, petit mal, and psychomotor.

The grand mal attack is the most severe. It

Epidemics of bubonic plague ("the black death") swept Europe repeatedly between the 14th and 17th centuries. Strange costumes like the above were worn to guard against infection.

is a form of convulsion, sometimes called a "fit." The person loses consciousness and may fall if he or she is not supported. The muscles jerk violently. The seizure lasts a few minutes, then the person may go into a deep sleep.

The petit mal attack is a milder form of seizure. The person may lose awareness, or "go blank." The seizure lasts for only a few seconds, and the person may not even realize he or she has had an attack. Most petit mal attacks occur in children.

During a psychomotor seizure, the person acts strangely for only a few minutes. Sometimes the person walks around aimlessly or tugs at his or her clothes.

Epileptic seizures may occur at any time. Some persons have frequent attacks; others have only a few. They seem to have no direct relationship to the emotional condition of the person.

Very little is known about the causes of epilepsy. It could be caused by brain damage due to infection, by physical injury, or by a tumor. Epilepsy, however, is not contagious.

Doctors treat epilepsy with certain drugs which reduce the seizures or eliminate them. With proper treatment, most epileptics can lead normal lives.   P.G.C./J.J.F.

EPIPHYTE (ep′ ə fīt′) An epiphyte is any plant that grows upon another plant for physical support. It is distinguished from a climbing plant which has roots in the ground, and from a parasitic plant which gets its food from its host. Epiphytes are often called air plants. They have specially modified roots and leaves which absorb water and minerals from moisture in the air. They have no attachment to the ground of other source of nutrients. Most epiphytes are tropical. These include orchids, ferns, and members of the cactus family. Some temperate varieties include mosses, liverworts, lichens, and algae. A.J.C./M.H.S.

EPITHELIUM (ep′ ə thē′ lē əm) Epithelium is an important living tissue found in human beings, some animals, and a few plants. It is made up of cells that are closely bound to each other to form sheets. Epithelial tissue has one or more of the following functions: protection, absorption, or secretion.

In human beings, epithelium covers the body and lines the passages of systems that open to the outside. In other words, epithelium lines the alimentary canal as well as the respiratory, reproductive, and excretory tracts.

There are three main types of epithelium, based on cell structure. Squamous epithelium is made of thin, flattened cells with irregular edges. It lines the mouth and esophagus, and is part of the skin. Cuboidal epithelium is made of small, boxlike cells. It lines some body cavities and helps make up some of the glands. Columnar epithelium has long, nar-

row, column-shaped cells. It lines most of the alimentary canal and makes up part of the skin. Some specialized columnar epithelial cells have hairlike structures called cilia. Cilia function to move fluids or other substances in one direction. Ciliated epithelium lines much of the respiratory system (bronchi, trachea, nasal passages), female reproductive system (fallopian tubes, uterus), and male reproductive system (vas deferens, epididymis). A.J.C./E.R.L.

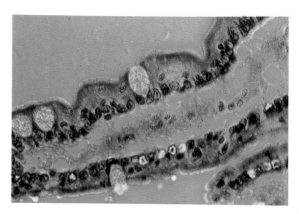

Epithelium is the cell tissue which forms the outer layer of the skin and the lining of most body cavities. Above, a greatly magnified cross-section of a villus, one of the thousands of tiny projections in the epithelium of the small intestine.

EPSOM SALT (ep′ səm sȯlt′) Epsom salt is a powdered form of magnesium sulfate. It is named for the springs in Epsom, England, where it was first obtained. It occurs dissolved in sea water and in most mineral waters. It also occurs in nature in association with minerals such as epsomite, gypsum, and limestone.

As a white powder, epsom salt is used as a laxative. Epsom salt can prevent the bowels (intestines) from absorbing water. Epsom salt should not be taken frequently. It interferes with the absorption of food materials. It should never be taken when there is abdominal pain.

Epsom salt is also mixed with water to make a solution for soaking inflamed body parts, especially the feet and hands.

J.J.A./A.D.

EQUATOR (i kwāt′ ər) The equator is an imaginary line around the middle of the earth, located halfway between the North and South Poles. The equator represents 0° latitude on a map. The equator is divided into 360° of longitude. (*See* LATITUDE AND LONGITUDE.)

Because of the slight bulge of the earth at the equator, the equatorial circumference (the length of the equator's circle) is a little longer than the polar circumference (the length of a circle around the earth which runs through both poles). At the equator, day and night are always 12 hours each.   J.M.C./W.R.S.

EQUILIBRIUM (ē′ kwə lib′ rē əm) Equilibrium is a state of rest or balance due to the equal action of opposing forces. When two or more forces acting on a body oppose or neutralize each other so that the body does not move, the forces are said to be in equilibrium. For example, at the exact time that the forward force of a football fullback is neutralized by the equal opposing force of a tackler, the forces are in equilibrium.

The ease with which the equilibrium of a body may be upset determines its type of equilibrium. If the center of gravity of an object must be raised in order to tilt it, the object is said to be in stable equilibrium. For example, a book lying on a table is in stable equilibrium. A pencil, balanced on a finger, is in unstable equilibrium. The slightest tipping of the pencil lowers its center of gravity, causing the knife to fall. A ball resting on a floor is in neutral equilibrium. Movements will neither raise nor lower its center of gravity.

A chemical equilibrium is a state of balance that is reached when chemical changes have apparently stopped. (*See* CHEMICAL REACTION.)   J.J.A./A.D.

EQUINOX (ē′ kwə näks′) The equinox is one of two days when the sun is directly over the equator at noon. The equinoxes usually occur on September 21 and March 21. On both these days, day and night are of equal length all over the world. The March 21 equinox is called the spring or vernal equinox because it signals the official start of spring in the northern hemisphere. September 21 is called the autumnal equinox because it is the first day of autumn in the northern hemisphere. *See also* SEASON; SOLSTICE.

    J.M.C./C.R.

EQUIVALENT (i kwiv′ ə lənt) The equivalent of a substance is an important measurement. It tells a chemist how much of that substance will combine or react with a set amount of another substance. The equivalent is also called the equivalent weight. It can be measured in grams. This is the gram-equivalent.

The equivalent of a substance is the number of grams that will combine with or displace one gram of hydrogen or eight grams of oxygen. One gram-equivalent of a substance will react with one gram-equivalent of another substance, or with a simple multiple or fraction of that amount.

For an element, the equivalent weight is found by dividing its atomic weight by its valence. *See also* CENTIMETER-GRAM-SECOND SYSTEM.   D.M.H.W./A.D.

ERBIUM (ər′ bē əm) Erbium is a metallic element. It belongs to the group of elements called the rare earths. Its chemical symbol is Er. It has an atomic number of 68 and an atomic weight of 167.3. Erbium melts at about 1,500°C [2,732°F] and boils at 2,510°C [4,550°F]. It has a valence of three. It forms rose-colored salts. It was named for the town of Ytterby in Sweden. It was discovered there in 1843 by the Swedish chemist Carl Mosander. It is found in the minerals gadolinite and euxenite.   D.M.H.W./J.R.W.

ERG (ərg) An erg is a unit of work, or energy, in the centimeter-gram-second (cgs) system of units. It equals the work done by a force of 1 dyne acting over a distance of 1 cm

[0.4 in]. An erg is also equal to one ten-millionth of a joule.   w.r.p./r.w.l.

EROSION (i rō′ zhən) Erosion is the gradual wearing down and carrying away of the earth's materials. Natural or geological erosion is a slow process caused by the weather, oceans, running water, wind, and ice. Soil erosion is sometimes the result of the abuse of land by people. (*See* WEATHERING.)

In geological erosion, the weather plays a major role. The wind is constantly wearing away rock, especially in dry areas. In moist areas, water fills the cracks in rocks. If the temperature falls below the freezing point, 0°C [32°F], the water freezes. Since ice occupies more space than water, the rocks are broken apart by the expanding ice. This rock debris may fall down cliffs or mountainsides, forming the piles of rock often seen along the seashore. These piles are called talus or scree.

Water is another important factor in erosion. Rivers carry pebbles, sand, and other debris that constantly rub against the river bed. The Grand Canyon in Arizona is a result of the erosion caused by the Colorado River. Some of the material carried by a river is deposited at its mouth, forming a delta.

Glaciers carry material from one location to another. When the glaciers retreated during the last ice age, they made significant changes in the landscape of the northern hemisphere. (*See* GLACIATION.)

Ocean waves pounding against the coast are constantly changing the shoreline. In some places, waves batter and erode the land. In other places, the eroded material is deposited to form new land.

Soil erosion may occur because people change the land, making it much more vulnerable to geological erosion. Natural vegetation, like forests and grasslands, holds the soil securely in place. When the vegetation is removed, the soil can be washed away by a heavy rainfall. Farm land is subject to severe erosion, especially in times of drought. *See also* GEOMORPHOLOGY.   j.m.c./w.r.s.

Sea erosion can sometimes wear even hard rock into strange shapes. Below, the Old Man of Hoy, a thin column of rock in the Orkney islands, Scotland, is the result of erosion. Erosion like this is a very slow process.

ESCALATOR (es′ kə lāt′ ər) An escalator is a moving stairway used in large stores and public buildings, like railroad, bus, and airline terminals. Passengers stand on steps mounted on an endless belt. The belt is driven by an electric motor. (*See* CONVEYOR.) The passengers are carried either up or down depending upon the direction the escalator is running. Escalators usually operate at a speed of about 0.61 m [2 ft] per second. At the top and the bottom, the steps fold to make a flat, moving platform which is level with the landing. This allows the passengers to step on and off the escalator easily. Moving handrails are on either side of the steps. They are usually made of rubber and canvas. The handrails move at the same speed as the steps.

An escalator can handle about ten times the hourly capacity of an average elevator. The first escalator was displayed in 1900 at the Paris Exposition by the Otis Elevator Company. In 1901, this machine was reinstalled at the Gimbel Brothers department store in Philadelphia, and was used until 1939.

W.R.P./R.W.L.

ESOPHAGUS (i säf′ ə gəs) The esophagus, or gullet, is a muscular tube in vertebrates that leads from the back of the mouth (pharynx) to the stomach. It is part of the alimentary canal. The esophagus is made of bands of circular and longitudinal muscles which contract in waves to force food into the stomach. These waves are called peristalsis. Although both striated and smooth muscles make up the esophagus, control of peristalsis is involuntary.

The length of the esophagus varies from animal to animal. A fish has a very short esophagus, while the giraffe has a long one. The esophagus of the bird is modified with a saclike storage structure called a crop. The human esophagus is located behind the trachea and is about 30 cm [12 in] long and about 2.5 cm [1 in] in diameter. It is able to stretch, however, to allow the passage of large particles of food. There are special sphincter muscles at both ends of the esophagus. When food enters the mouth, it is mixed with saliva. The esophageal sphincter, located between the pharynx and the esophagus, opens, lets the food in, and closes again to keep the food from backing up into the mouth. Lubrication is added by mucus-secreting glands along the esophagus as peristalsis pushes the food through. The cardiac sphincter, located between the esophagus and the stomach, opens, letting food pass into the stomach. The sphincter then closes to prevent gastric fluids in the stomach from entering the esophagus. Heartburn is a condition caused by gastric juice in the esophagus.

Some animals, such as ruminants, are able to cause the esophagus to undergo a reverse peristalsis. This brings food from the stomach back up into the mouth. This returned food, or cud, is chewed and swallowed again.

A.J.C./J.J.F.

Left, the ester isoamyl acetate has the smell of bananas. Isoamyl acetate can be made synthetically to give banana flavor to ice cream and toothpaste, among other substances.

ESTER (es′ tər) Esters are a group of chemical compounds. They are formed by the reaction of an alcohol with an acid. Esters are organic chemicals. (*See* COMPOUND; ORGANIC CHEMISTRY.) All acids contain an acidic hydrogen atom. This atom can be replaced by a metal to form a salt. Or it can be replaced by an organic hydrocarbon group to form an ester.

An example of an ester is ethyl acetate. It is made by acetic acid reacting with ethanol.

Ethanol is an alcohol. It is also called ethyl alcohol. In ethyl acetate, the ethyl group replaces the acidic hydrogen in acetic acid.

Many esters have a pleasant odor. The flavor of fruits and the perfumes of flowers are caused mainly by esters. Esters are used as solvents and in manufacturing other chemicals. They are also used as artificial flavors and perfumes.   M.E./J.M.

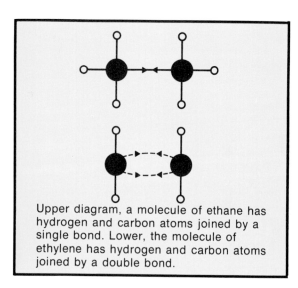

Upper diagram, a molecule of ethane has hydrogen and carbon atoms joined by a single bond. Lower, the molecule of ethylene has hydrogen and carbon atoms joined by a double bond.

ETHANE (eth′ ān′) Ethane (C_2H_6) is a colorless and odorless gas. It is found in natural gas and in coal gas. Its boiling point is −89°C [−128°F]. It is used in industry for making other chemical compounds. Ethane is a hydrocarbon because its molecule contains only hydrogen and carbon atoms. *See also* HYDRO-CARBON.   M.E./J.M.

ETHER (ē′ thər) Ether ($C_2H_5OC_2H_5$) is a pleasant-smelling liquid. It boils at 34.5°C [94.1° F]. Its vapor is very flammable. Ether must, therefore, be handled very carefully and kept well away from flames. Ether is made by ethanol reacting with sulfuric acid. Ether is used as an anaesthetic. It is also widely used in industry for dissolving waxes, oils, and other products.

Chemists use the word ether to mean a group of chemical compounds. They call the ether described above diethyl ether. Ethers

always have two hydrocarbon groups attached to an oxygen atom.   M.E./J.M.

ETHYLENE (eth′ ə lēn′) Ethylene (C_2H_4) is a colorless gas with a faint smell resembling ether. It is made by removing some of the hydrogen from ethane. It is also obtained by refining petroleum. Ethylene is used as an anaesthetic, a fuel, and in making other chemicals. It also helps to ripen fruit. In a molecule of ethylene, the two carbon atoms are joined together by a double bond. (*See* BOND, CHEMICAL.) Its formula can be written as $CH_2\!\!=\!\!CH_2$.

A large amount of ethylene is used to make polyethylene. In order to make polyethylene, ethylene is polymerized. (*See* POLYMERIZATION.) This splits open the double bond, and long chains of CH_2 groups are formed. Chemists sometimes call ethylene ethene.   M.E./J.M.

Above, an ethylene producing plant located in Grangemouth, Scotland.

EUCALYPTUS (yü′ kə lip′ təs) Eucalyptus is a genus with more than 500 species of tall, fast-growing trees. Native to Australia, these members of the myrtle family grow in warm, moist regions throughout the world. Some

Eucalyptus leaves and buds are the sole source of food of the koala bear.

species grow as tall as 100 m [330 ft]. The most common variety found in the United States is the blue gum eucalyptus (*Eucalyptus globulus*). This tree is cultivated in Florida, California, and Texas, and is frequently grown as a windbreaker around orchards of citrus trees. Like all eucalyptus, it has long, thick leaves and nectar-filled flowers which grow in the axils.

Eucalyptus is an important source of lumber and is used for telephone poles, ships, and railroad ties. The bark is a source of tannin which is used in some medicines, and of a resin called Botany Bay kino which can be used to protect wood from worms. The leaves are rich in an oil which can be used as a stimulant, a deodorant, and an antiseptic.
A.J.C./M.H.S.

EUROPIUM (yu̇ rō′ pē əm) Europium (Eu) is a silvery white metallic element. It has an atomic number of 63 and an atomic weight of 151.96. The melting point of europium is around 822°C [1,512°F]. Its boiling point is

1,597°C [2,907°F]. Its relative density is 5.3. It belongs to a group of metals with very similar properties, called the alkaline earths. Europium was first discovered in 1901 by the French chemist Eugène Demarçay. He named it after the continent of Europe.

Europium occurs in the minerals bastnaesite and monazite. These minerals also contain a number of other alkaline earth metals. Europium is used to make control rods for nuclear reactors. These rods are used to control the speed of the nuclear reaction. Compounds of europium are used in color television screens. They are responsible for producing the color red.   M.E./J.R.W.

EUTROPHICATION See SUCCESSION.

EVAPORATION (i vap' ə rā' shən) Evaporation occurs when a substance changes from a liquid or solid state into a vapor or gas. The form of a substance depends on the temperature or the amount of pressure it is subjected to. For example, water in a dish in a warm room may soon dry up. Wet clothes hung on a clothesline on a dry sunny day lose their moisture in a short time. Heat in the air changes the water in the dish and the clothes to water vapor. The warmer and drier the air, the more rapidly evaporation goes on.

Evaporation takes place from the surface of a liquid at any temperature. It also takes place from solids. Ice and snow send off vapor. This can be observed a day or two after a snowstorm. The snow disappears, even though the temperature has never gone above freezing. The water evaporates directly from the solid without first becoming a liquid. The formation of vapor in this way is called sublimation.

Evaporation in plants is called transpiration. Plants absorb moisture through their roots. They lose the moisture by evaporation through their leaves. The more leaf surface exposed, the more rapid the transpiration.

When a liquid evaporates from the surface of an object, that surface becomes much cooler because it requires heat to change a liquid into a vapor or gas. For example, sponging a fevered patient with alcohol reduces body temperature. Heat is drawn from the body by evaporation of the alcohol. In this sense, evaporation is a cooling process.

In some large areas, the process of evaporation is vital to plant and animal life. Water evaporates from oceans, rivers, the moist earth, or ponds and lakes and later falls as rain on these areas. (See CLOUD; RAIN.)

Other substances, such as ether and ammonia, evaporate much more rapidly than water. The rapid evaporation of ammonia requires much heat and is important in refrigerators. See also VOLATILE LIQUID.

J.J.A./AD.

The evening primrose is one of more than 500 species of flowering plants which belong to the evening primrose family. This family also includes the popular fuchsias.

EVENING PRIMROSE FAMILY (ēv' ning prim' rōz') The evening primrose family includes more than 500 species of herbaceous plants and shrubs. They grow throughout North America and in parts of Europe. The most common evening primrose, *Oenothera biennis*, is a wild flower that grows as tall as 1.8 m [6 ft]. It has hairy, stalkless leaves measuring about 15 cm [6 in] long. The flowers are usually large, about 10 cm [4 in] wide, and may be bright yellow, white, or pink. See also FUCHSIA.   J.J.A./A.D.